Qualifications and Credit Framework (QCF)
LEVEL 2 CERTIFICATE IN ACCOUNTING

WORKBOOK

Working Effectively in
Accounting and
Finance

2011 Edition

First edition 2010
Second edition June 2011

ISBN 9780 7517 9772 5
(Previous ISBN 9780 7517 8576 0)

British Library Cataloguing-in-Publication Data
A catalogue record for this book is available from the British
Library

Published by

BPP Learning Media Ltd
BPP House
Aldine Place
London
W12 8AA

www.bpp.com/learningmedia

Printed in the United Kingdom

CONTENTS

Introduction (v)

Assessment Strategy (vii)

Study Guide x

1   Introduction 1

2   The role of the financial functions 7

3   The organisational framework 23

4   Communication skills 43

5   Presenting information 63

6   Working independently 89

7   Working as part of a team 115

8   Developing skills and knowledge 133

Answers to chapter tasks 153

Test your learning – answers 169

AAT Sample assessment 193

AAT Sample assessment – answers 205

AAT Practice assessment 213

AAT Practice assessment – answers 223

Index 229

A NOTE ABOUT COPYRIGHT

INTRODUCTION

Since July 2010 the AAT's assessments have fallen within the **Qualifications and Credit Framework** and most papers are now assessed by way of an on demand **computer based assessment**. BPP Learning Media has invested heavily to produce new ground breaking market leading resources. In particular, our **online question banks** ensure that students are prepared for online testing by means of an online environment where tasks mimic the style of the AAT's assessment tasks.

The BPP range of resources comprises:

- **Texts**, covering all the knowledge and understanding needed by students, with numerous illustrations of 'how it works', practical examples and tasks for students to use to consolidate their learning. The majority of tasks within the texts have been written in an interactive style that reflects the style of the online tasks the AAT will set. Texts are available in our traditional paper format and, in addition, as ebooks which can be downloaded to your PC or laptop.

- **Question Banks**, including additional learning questions plus the AAT's practice assessment and a number of other full practice assessments. Full answers to all questions and assessments, prepared by BPP Learning Media Ltd, are included. Our question banks are provided **free of charge** in an online environment which mimics the AAT's testing environment. This enables you to familiarise yourself with the environment in which you will be tested.

- **Passcards**, which are handy pocket-sized revision tools designed to fit in a handbag or briefcase to enable you to revise anywhere at anytime. All major points are covered in the passcards which have been designed to assist you in consolidating knowledge.

- **Workbooks**, which have been designed to cover the units that are assessed by way of project/case study. The workbooks contain many practical tasks to assist in the learning process and also a sample assessment or project to work through.

- **Lecturers' resources**, providing a further bank of tasks, answers and full practice assessments for classroom use, available separately only to lecturers whose colleges adopt BPP Learning Media material. The lecturers' resources are available in both paper format and online in e format. What fantastic news: you can now give your students an online mock.

This Workbook for *Working Effectively in Accounting and Finance* has been written specifically to ensure comprehensive yet concise coverage of the AAT's new learning outcomes and assessment criteria. It is fully up-to-date as at June 2011 and reflects both the AAT's unit guide and the practice assessment provided by the AAT.

Each chapter contains:

- Clear, step-by-step explanation of the topic

- Logical progression and linking from one chapter to the next

- Numerous illustrations of 'how it works'

- Interactive tasks within the text of the chapter itself, with answers at the back of the book. These tasks have been written in the style that you will see in the real assessments

- Test your learning questions of varying complexity, again with answers supplied at the back of the book.

The emphasis in all tasks and test questions is on the practical application of the skills acquired.

If you have any comments about this book, please e-mail suedexter@bpp.com or write to Sue Dexter, Publishing Director, BPP Learning Media Ltd, BPP House, Aldine Place, London W12 8AA.

VAT

You will find examples and questions in this Workbook which need you to calculate or be aware of a rate of VAT. This is stated at 20% in these examples and questions.

ASSESSMENT STRATEGY

Working Effectively in Accounting and Finance (WEAF) is a skills unit where learners are required to demonstrate they have the skills to be able to work effectively in an organisation. Working practices will vary between organisations and as such learners will be required to demonstrate that these skills are transferable to all organisations.

The assessment for this unit will therefore be case study based to ensure that all learners, whether currently working in an accounting environment or not, will be able to demonstrate the necessary skills.

The assessment is expected to be taken in two two-hour sessions. Each session has 15 minutes reading time. A maximum gap of two weeks is permitted between each session.

The assessment will be divided into the two sessions as follows.

Session A

- Explain the role of accountancy or payroll and other financial functions within the business

- Identify the contribution of those in accounting or payroll and other financial roles to an organisation

- Identify your appropriate reporting lines within your working environment

- Recognise any organisational policies and procedures that affect your work

- Plan and manage your own workload effectively and prioritise tasks

- Identify the impact that the completion or non-completion of your work can have on colleagues

- Resolve or refer conflicts or dissatisfaction within your working environment

Session B

- Explain the importance of CPD and identify your own development needs and objectives

- Monitor and review your own development needs and objectives

Session A or Session B

- Demonstrate a level of numeracy skills appropriate to your role within the organisation

- Demonstrate a level of literacy skills appropriate to your role within the organisation

- Present information in an informal business report (including diagrams) format and within organisational guidelines

- Present information in an email or memo format and within organisational guidelines

Learners will be required to complete tasks, based upon a case study.

The learner's completed answers to the set tasks will be presented for assessment in the form of a computer file. As part of this unit is about communication, literacy and numeracy skills, the presentation (including grammar, spelling, use of business language) of the finished work is extremely important and will be assessed together with the content of the answers.

The assessment material will normally be provided by the AAT, delivered online and assessed locally. Learners will be required to demonstrate competence in both sections of the assessment.

It is recommended that *Basic Accounting I* and *II* and *Basic Costing* are studied and taken before *WEAF*.

Competency

For the purpose of assessment the competency level for AAT assessment is set at 70 per cent. The level descriptor in the table below describes the ability and skills students at this level must successfully demonstrate to achieve competence.

QCF Level descriptor	Summary
	Achievement at level 2 reflects the ability to select and use relevant knowledge, ideas, skills and procedures to complete well-defined tasks and address straightforward problems. It includes taking responsibility for completing tasks and procedures and exercising autonomy and judgement subject to overall direction or guidance.
	Knowledge and understanding
	■ Use understanding of facts, procedures and ideas to complete well-defined tasks and address straightforward problems
	■ Interpret relevant information and ideas
	■ Be aware of the types of information that are relevant to the area of study or work
	Application and action
	■ Complete well-defined, generally routine tasks and address straightforward problems
	■ Select and use relevant skills and procedures
	■ Identify, gather and use relevant information to inform actions
	■ Identify how effective actions have been
	Autonomy and accountability
	■ Take responsibility for completing tasks and procedures
	■ Exercise autonomy and judgement subject to overall direction or guidance

AAT UNIT GUIDE

Work Effectively in Accounting and Finance (WEAF)

Introduction

Please read this document in conjunction with the standards for all relevant units.

The purpose of the unit

This unit is about gaining a range of transferable skills which will enable the learner to work effectively within an accounting environment. It aims to prove a reasonable standard of literacy and numeracy skills which is essential for the workplace.

Learning objectives

The learner develops an understanding of how to work within the accounting/payroll environment and of what is expected of them at this level. They will develop an insight into how their role interacts with others and how they are expected to communicate within business with effective results.

Learning outcomes

The unit consists of four learning outcomes which in turn comprise a number of assessment criteria.

QCF unit	Learning outcome	Assessment criteria	Covered in Chapter
Work Effectively in Accounting and Finance	Understand the accounting or payroll function within an organisation	Explain the role of accounting or payroll and other financial functions within the business	2
		Identify the contribution of those in accounting or payroll and other financial roles to maintaining the smooth running, solvency and legal compliance of an organisation.	
		Identify your appropriate reporting lines within your working environment	3
		Recognise any organisation policies and procedures that affect your work	3

QCF unit	Learning outcome	Assessment criteria	Covered in Chapter
	Demonstrate a range of effective communication skills	Demonstrate a level of numeracy and literacy skills appropriate to your role within the organisation.	4
		Present information in appropriate formats and within organisational guidelines for:	5
		Informal business report (including diagrams)	
		Letter	
		E-mail or memo	
	Work independently or as part of a team	Plan and manage your own workload effectively and prioritise tasks	6
		Identify the impact that the completion or non-completion of your work can have on colleagues	7
		Resolve or refer conflicts or dissatisfaction within your working environment	7
	Develop skills and knowledge to meet personal and organisational needs	Explain the importance of continuing professional development and identify your own development needs and objectives.	8
		Monitor and review your own development needs and objectives	

Delivery guidance: Work effectively in accounting and finance

1 Understand the accounting or payroll function within an organisation

1.1 Explain the role of accounting or payroll and other financial functions within the business.

- The role of accountancy, payroll or financial functions within the business is one of providing a service to other departments within the organisation. These functions provide other departments with information on the financial implications of their activities including the employment of staff.

- Learners should be aware that the primary role of the staff of the accountancy, payroll and finance functions is to provide complete, accurate and timely information and support the other functions within the organisation.

1.2 Identify the contribution of those in accounting or payroll and other financial roles to maintaining the smooth running, solvency and legal compliance of an organisation.

- The information provided by these functions should be complete, accurate and timely for it to be of maximum benefit to the smooth running of an organisation.

- Learners should be aware of the contribution the accountancy, payroll and finance functions make to the success of the organisation as a whole.

- Learners should have an understanding of how the accountancy, payroll and finance functions manage working capital and ensure the organisation remains solvent. The accounting and payroll functions have a very important role in ensuring an organisation can meet its debts as they fall due (solvency). They will provide information to an organisation about the cash flow implications of its activities and when debts have to be repaid. The management of working capital (day-to-day funds) is an important role of the accounting and payroll functions.

- In addition to providing information to all departments within an organisation the accounting and payroll functions will ensure that all regulatory requirements for the preparation of financial and payroll records and information are adhered to in order that future liabilities (fines and remedial work) are minimised. Payroll and accounting staff are required to ensure their working practices comply with legislative requirements (NB knowledge of specific legislation is NOT required). The learner must understand that they need to follow procedures to protect the safety and security of themselves and others, ensure confidentiality is preserved and the procedures for the secure storage of data and information.

1.3 Identify your reporting lines within your working environment.

- Organisations will vary in the reporting lines applicable to their staff. It is important for everyone in the organisation to understand the people within their organisation to which they report. It may be that they have a designated supervisor/line manager or they may have to report to different people (eg line manager, supervisor, colleagues, training manager) within the organisation dependent upon the task.

1.4 Recognise any organisational policies and procedures that affect your work.

- Organisational policies and procedures influence most aspects of working practices. The importance of ensuring that working practices and standards comply with the organisation's requirements must be understood and its role in an efficient organisation. Policies and procedures will include (but are not limited to) departmental deadlines, authorisation procedures, designated signatories, maintenance of their working area and secure storage of data and information.

2 Demonstrate a range of effective communication skills

2.1 Demonstrate a level of numeracy and literacy skills appropriate to your role within the organisation.

- The learner will be able to communicate effectively using business communications including informal business reports, letters, e-mails and memos. Clear and concise communication creates greater efficiency in an organisation and learners are required to demonstrate literacy skills which would be expected of a Level 2 Accounting Technician.

- Learners will be required to ensure the document is professionally presented, the content is technically correct and it is clearly understandable and projects the appropriate corporate image.

- Learners must be able to demonstrate that business language is more formal than everyday language.

- The learner will have the numeracy skills required of a Level 2 Accounting Technician. They will be required to use relevant skills including (but not confined to) addition, subtraction, multiplication, division, percentages, fractions and rounding to a set number of decimal places.

2.2 Present information in appropriate formats and within organisational guidelines for:

- Informal business reports (including diagrams)
- Letter
- Email or memo

- The ability to produce informal business reports, letters, emails and memos is an important skill for the learner at this level. Understanding the requirements of the recipient improves the clarity of communication and leads to more effective relationships.

- The production of hand written and word processed business reports (including diagrams), memos, letters and e-mails will be required and both the format and content is assessable. These will be expected to be presented professionally, correctly use the subject line where applicable, include content which is technically correct and clearly understandable and they must project the correct image for the organisation.

- It should be remembered to keep the content short and simple by:
    - Ensuring it is well structured
    - Making it easy to read
    - Being unambiguous
    - Avoiding the use of jargon
    - Eliminating unnecessary words
    - Including appropriate diagrams

3   Work independently or as part of a team

3.1 Plan and manage your own workload effectively and prioritise tasks.

- Learners will be required to demonstrate they have the necessary skills to work independently and manage their own workload effectively in order that outcomes are achieved in the most efficient manner. While completing work the importance of planning and prioritising tasks, adhering to agreed working practices, respecting confidentiality and meeting agreed deadlines must be fully understood. Learners will be able to select and use the most appropriate planning aids including, but not confined to, schedules, diaries, to do lists and action plans.

- Learners will be required to show how they meet deadlines, prioritise and re-prioritise tasks within their workload, maintain confidentiality and how they communicate with their line manager/supervisor. It is important that staff keep their colleagues/supervisors or line managers informed of their progress against deadlines and if a deadline is not met they will need to communicate this effectively to their supervisor/line manager at the earliest opportunity.

3.2 Identify the impact that the completion or non-completion of your work can have on colleagues.

- In any organisation staff do not work in isolation and the contribution the completion/non-completion of their work has on the whole team/ department is an important aspect of organisational efficiency. When work is not completed by individuals the negative effect this can have on the team, in terms of the transfer of work to others and on working relationships, must be understood.

- Learners will understand their contribution to team work and the implications for other members of the team if they do not complete tasks.

- Learners will identify the importance of meeting deadlines and the procedures to follow if unexpected problems are encountered.

- Learners will need to understand the importance of working as a team and their role in the team achieving its objectives.

3.3 Resolve or refer conflicts of dissatisfaction within your working environment.

- Conflict as a result of working styles or personality can occur within any team and a basic understanding of the causes and the types of conflict which impact upon team performance is required. Staff must understand the circumstances when they can resolve a conflict of dissatisfaction and the circumstances when and to whom they have to refer issues which they cannot resolve.

- The damaging effects of conflict and dissatisfaction on an organisation must be appreciated alongside how effective conflict/dissatisfaction management can contribute to better team work and more productive working relationships. Learners should be able to suggest ways of resolving conflict and, where this is not possible, how and to whom to refer the issue.

4 Develop skills and knowledge to meet personal and organisational needs

4.1 Explain the importance of continuing professional development and identify your own development needs and objectives.

- Continuing Professional Development (CPD) is an important requirement for every member of the accounting and payroll departments. It is the responsibility of every individual to maintain CPD appropriate to their current job role and their career aspirations. The sources of CPD (including but not limited to technical updates, training courses/seminars, research, internet, publications) available and the requirement to record CPD must be fully understood.

- Learners should know how to identify their own development needs and objectives on a formal basis and the need to include their supervisor/line manager in this process. It is important to be able to set clear SMART (Specific, Measurable, Achievable, Realistic, Timely) objectives which are agreed with the supervisor/line manager.

4.2 Monitor and review your own development needs and objectives.

- After setting SMART objectives staff should be able to monitor and review their progress against these objectives on a regular basis. This may involve seeking feedback from colleagues/line manager and assessing their performance against given criteria.

- The effect the development of staff skills and knowledge has on improving organisational efficiency and in helping to meet targets must be understood in order that CPD is seen by all as an investment rather than a burden.

chapter 1:
INTRODUCTION

---
chapter coverage 📖

In this chapter, we look at the information you are likely to be provided with in the assessment and the tasks you may be expected to perform. We then set out the approach you should take in order to pass the assessment and the ways in which the Workbook will help you.

The topics covered are:

✍ Your assessment

✍ Passing your assessment

✍ How this Workbook will enable you to pass

YOUR ASSESSMENT

Your assessment will consist of a case study SCENARIO together with a number of tasks for you to perform.

The assessment is split into two two-hour assessments. They must be sat within two weeks of each other.

Your answers to the tasks will be presented for assessment in a computer file. The standard of presentation (including grammar, spelling, use of business language) of your work is very important and will be assessed together with the content of your answers.

The case study scenario

The scenario will provide details of an imaginary organisation and set out who you are, for the purposes of the assessment, within that organisation. The information provided is likely to include:

- A description of the department in which you work and of your role in that department

- A diagram, known as an ORGANISATION CHART, indicating the people you work with, their job titles and their level of seniority within the organisation

- Descriptions of the roles performed by some of the people you work with.

Once you have read this information you will be able to imagine that you are the character in the assessment and that you work for the organisation described.

The assessment will also include a number of documents. These documents will contain the information that you will use in order to carry out the tasks. Documents provided in the AAT practice assessment include:

- Details of the organisation's policy in relation to expense claims

- Work request forms showing the work that you have been asked to carry out

- A schedule of the cost and timing of proposed training for the staff in your department.

There are six pages of information in the AAT practice assessment.

The tasks

The assessment will require you to carry out a number of tasks: there are 13 tasks in the AAT practice assessment. Particular tasks may require you to:

- Explain something: the first three tasks in the practice assessment are examples of this type of task.

- Write a letter, an informal report, an email or a memo. Tasks 1.1e, 2.1a and 2.1e in the practice assessment are examples of this type of task.

- Analyse numerical information provided in the assessment: Task 2.1b in the practice assessment is an example of this type of task.

When carrying out some of the tasks you will need to imagine that you are the character in the assessment but that you possess your own personal characteristics, for example your own professional strengths and weaknesses. Tasks 2.1c and 2.1d in the practice assessment are examples of tasks requiring you to think in this way.

The AAT practice assessment is included in this Workbook – have a quick look at it before you read the rest of this chapter.

PASSING THE ASSESSMENT

The assessment will require you to demonstrate that you have the skills necessary to work effectively in an organisation.

Before you sit the assessment

Before you sit the assessment you will need to:

- Read and understand the contents of this Workbook

- Carry out the tasks within each chapter and answer the questions at the end of each chapter so that you have practised the types of task you may be asked to carry out

- Develop your communication and numeracy skills where necessary.

Sitting the assessment

When you sit the assessment you will need to:

- Read the scenario carefully so that you have a clear understanding of who you are and the organisation for which you work

- Read each task carefully and ensure that you do precisely what is asked; just as you would in a real working environment

- Prepare your answers to the tasks as neatly and professionally as you can.

HOW THIS WORKBOOK WILL ENABLE YOU TO PASS

The purpose of this Workbook is to enable you to pass the assessment. Accordingly, it:

- Contains the technical information you need.

- Explains the relevance of the information that may be provided to you in the assessment and how to use the various documents that you are likely to see

- Explains the different documents you may be expected to produce in the assessment

- Sets out the skills you need to develop and suggests ways of improving your performance

- Contains tasks within each chapter, and 'test your learning' questions at the end of each chapter, which will provide you with the opportunity to test your understanding and practise tasks similar to those that you are likely to see in the assessment.

CHAPTER OVERVIEW

- The scenario in the assessment will place you in an imaginary organisation with a defined role, colleagues and tasks to perform.

- Likely tasks include explaining something, preparing letters, emails or other documents and analysing numerical information.

- Before you sit the assessment you will need to be familiar with the contents of this Workbook and to have developed your skills.

- When you sit the assessment you must take the same degree of care as you would in your real working environment.

- This Workbook contains everything you need to pass the assessment.

Keywords

Scenario – an imaginary setting consisting of an organisation and its employees, one of which is you

Organisation chart – a diagram depicting the formal structure of an organisation (covered in detail in Chapter 3)

chapter 2:
THE ROLE OF THE FINANCIAL FUNCTIONS

chapter coverage 📖

This chapter introduces the role of accounting, payroll and other financial functions within an organisation, and explores the various ways in which those individuals in financial roles contribute to business objectives.

It consists principally of information that you may need to refer to when carrying out the tasks in your assessment.

The topics covered are:

✍ Functions within an organisation

✍ The financial functions

✍ Contribution to business objectives

✍ The legal framework

FUNCTIONS WITHIN AN ORGANISATION

An organisation may perform a number of different activities in pursuit of its objectives, depending on what type of organisation it is. These activities may include:

- The research, design and development of products and services (R & D)

- Production (in a manufacturing organisation) or other operational activities (such as providing services)

- The marketing and selling of products or services to customers

- The development and use of information technology systems for the business (IT)

- The purchasing or procurement of materials and supplies used in the business

- The warehousing, transport and distribution of finished products (sometimes called 'logistics')

- The management of the organisation's staff or 'human resources' (HR)

- Administrative and clerical activities supporting the running of the business

- The management of the organisation's finances and financial information (accounting and finance).

Some of these functions, known as LINE FUNCTIONS, are directly involved in the main service-delivering or revenue-earning activity of the business: they directly fulfil the organisation's primary purpose and objectives. Examples include the production, marketing, sales and distribution functions.

Other functions, known as STAFF FUNCTIONS, exist to *support* the line functions in fulfilling their objectives: providing them with the resources, systems and information they need to perform their activities efficiently and effectively. Examples include IT, HR, administration – and accounting and finance.

THE FINANCIAL FUNCTIONS

You may already have some grasp of the role and tasks of the accounting and payroll functions from your work, or studies for other Units. However, it may be helpful to have an overview here, with a particular focus on how accounting and payroll 'fit' within the organisation as a whole.

The accounting function

The role of the accounting function is to support the organisation's other functions by compiling, preparing and providing complete, accurate and timely information on all financial aspects of the business. Business accounting is the process of:

- recording all financial transactions carried out by an organisation, and

- summarising the transactions to present a financial picture which supports both:

  - accountability to investors and other external interested parties (or 'stakeholders'), and

  - internal management decision-making about the business.

Financial accounting

FINANCIAL ACCOUNTING is mainly concerned with the processing and recording of transactions (book-keeping), and the production of financial statements for users outside the business.

The financial accounts function firstly records transactions between the business and its customers, suppliers, employees and owners, using a system of nominal, sales and purchases ledgers and taxation records. These records then enable any business of any size, from a 'one man band' sole trader to a large professional partnership or company, to prepare its financial statements:

- a balance sheet (known under international accounting standards as a statement of financial position or SFP)

- a profit and loss account (known under international accounting standards as an income statement or IS) and

- other primary financial statements and notes if required.

The law requires the financial statements of companies in particular:

- to be presented in compliance with detailed regulations;

- to be audited, where necessary (to ensure that they represent a true and fair picture of the financial position of the company); and

- to be lodged with a government official called the Registrar of Companies, so that they can be made available to suppliers, investors and other interested parties.

Similarly, taxation records of all businesses must be compiled according to detailed rules, and submitted to HM Revenue and Customs.

Management accounting

MANAGEMENT ACCOUNTING is mainly concerned with the production of financial reports to assist managers in all the business's functions in

- measuring performance
- making decisions and
- generally running the business.

Management accounts are not regulated by law: managers can ask for whatever records and reports they think will be helpful to them: unlike financial accounts, these are purely internal documents, and, for commercial reasons, are mostly kept strictly confidential.

Management accountants perform activities such as cost analysis, cost control, budget preparation and budgetary control (monitoring actual performance against budgeted performance).

Information flows to and from the accounting function

The accounts department needs to receive information from all the other departments of the organisation, in order to compile reports and records on the financial implications of their activities. Examples include: cost estimates; production schedules; expenses claim forms; records of staff work and overtime hours (eg timesheets or clock cards); changes to staff details (eg pay grades, leave arrangements, promotions); invoices to process and pay; purchase orders and goods received notes to check against invoices – and so on.

In return, the accounts department provides information to all the departments of the organisation on the financial implications of their activities: wage/salary costs; current costs against expected budgeted costs; depreciation charges on assets; expenses; cash flow summaries; customer debts (for the sales or credit control department); revenue and profit forecasts; and so on.

Payroll

The payroll function may be a section of the accounting function. It is concerned solely with payroll processing, including tasks such as: the calculation of gross pay from salary data and timesheets etc; the calculation of tax, National Insurance and other deductions; preparing payslips; making appropriate returns to external agencies such as HM Revenue and Customs; making up wage packets with cash, or preparing data for direct credit (BACS); distributing payslips to employees; preparing payroll statistics.

Task 1

From what we have just said about the tasks performed by the payroll function, see if you can give some examples of:

(a) Information *required* by the payroll department *from* the HR department and other departments where people are employed.

(b) Information *provided* by the payroll department to other internal and external parties.

This is an example of a task that you could be asked to carry out in your assessment.

Other financial functions

An organisation may have separate sections for other (or more specific) aspects of finance, such as:

- Cash administration and money-handling tasks, such as cashiers, petty cash and banking

- Financing (eg managing loans and other sources of finance)

- Taxation.

The financial functions as service and support providers

It is important to realise that people in finance do not work in isolation. Whatever their specific tasks, the financial functions as a whole provide a *service* to all the other functions in the organisation: supporting them in the fulfilment of their objectives – and through them, the objectives of the organisation as a whole. The 'customers' of the financial function include all of the other functions in the organisation.

Financial information

The main role of the accounting and payroll functions is to support managers and staff in other functions by preparing and providing complete, accurate and timely information on the *financial implications of their activities*.

The accounting function provides information about the financial implications of operational activities such as holding inventory (stock), making sale and purchase transactions. The accounting function shows:

- what the activities cost (both immediately and over time);

- what revenues, returns or benefits they earn;

- what the balance is between cash coming into and cash going out of the business (CASH FLOW); and

- what the cash flow situation means for:

  - the availability of day-to-day finance to maintain organisational activity (this is the WORKING CAPITAL required by the business) and

  - the ability of the organisation to pay its debts when they fall due (its SOLVENCY).

For other functions of the organisation, this information highlights important decision factors such as:

- what they can afford to spend
- what they need to earn
- how profitable and efficient their activities are, and
- where their profitability or efficiency may need to be improved.

The payroll function similarly provides information about the financial implications of employing people:

- how much cash is needed to pay them

- how much it costs to keep the organisation staffed and operating, and

- whether there is potential to increase – or a need to decrease – staffing or staff costs.

Accounting information therefore supports managers in making sound decisions about the resources available to them. It equips managers for:

- PLANNING: helping them to understand the financial implications of their planned activities; what resources are or are not available to implement them (ie whether their planned activities are affordable); and their potential costs and benefits in financial terms (ie whether the planned activities are cost-effective and worthwhile).

- CONTROL: helping them to measure the results of their activities against their plans; whether they came in 'on budget' (in line with anticipated costs); whether they earned the expected revenues and profits; whether resources were efficiently used; and so on.

Complete, accurate and timely information

In fulfilling this service role, the important thing for the finance function is not the quantity of information but its *quality*. In order to be of maximum benefit to the organisation, the information provided must be complete, accurate and timely;

- *Complete*: including all data relevant to the purpose for which the information will be used

- *Accurate*: factually and numerically correct, and to an appropriate level of detail for the purpose for which the information will be used

- *Timely:* delivered at the right time for the information to be meaningful and used to support decision-making and action.

CONTRIBUTION TO BUSINESS OBJECTIVES

We have looked at what the financial functions broadly 'do' within the business: that is, their *role*. But why is this important? What does it *contribute* to the fulfilment of business objectives and the success of the organisation as a whole?

By providing financial information to all functions and departments within an organisation, those in accounting, payroll and other financial roles make an important contribution in three key areas:

- The smooth running and efficiency of the business
- The working capital and solvency of the business
- The legal compliance of the business.

Smooth running and efficiency

Information is the life blood of all business activity. The financial functions play an important role in the smooth running of the organisation, through supplying high-quality, timely information to support managers in their decision-making.

Organisational EFFICIENCY is about achieving objectives with the minimum use of resources (particularly, the minimum *unnecessary* expenditure or waste).

The financial functions support efficiency by providing information for planning (so that resources are not used thoughtlessly) and control (so that the use of resources is checked, and managers are held accountable for how they are used).

- In collaboration with other department managers, the accounting function produces annual budgets and long-term plans, which act as guidelines and benchmarks for measuring the performance of different departments, and the organisation as a whole.

- They periodically provide departments with information on how they are *actually performing* or progressing, for comparison against the benchmarks set out in plans and budgets.

- This enables departments to *measure* how effectively and efficiently they are operating, and to identify areas where performance and efficiency can be *improved* – or where forecasts and plans may need to be adjusted to be more realistic.

Working capital and solvency

The accounting function has a very important role in managing WORKING CAPITAL: the day-to-day finance which is used to keep the business running. Working capital basically comprises:

Inventory (stock)		Payables (creditors)
Receivables (debtors)	LESS	Overdrafts
Cash		

The accounting function provides information to other departments about the CASH FLOW implications of their activities: what money is flowing into the organisation and when (in income) and what money is flowing out of the organisation and when (in expenditure), and the balance between these two flows at any given time. The organisation and its various functions can then:

- Know what working capital is available for use at any given time

- Ensure there is an adequate cash balance at any given time by managing:

  - the level of inventory (stock), by ensuring that no more is held than is necessary

  - the collection of receipts from receivables (debtors), by operating a strict credit control policy,

- the making of payments to payables (creditors), by negotiating favourable credit terms

■ Plan to earn extra revenue, or to raise finance (eg by taking out a loan or selling assets), if required to maintain adequate reserves of working capital.

By closely monitoring the cash balances of the business, the accounting function also has a very important role in ensuring the SOLVENCY of the organisation: that is, its ability to meet its short-term and long-term debts as they fall due.

The accounting function provides information to the organisation about:

■ Debts that are owing and when they have to be paid

■ The availability of cash to cover debts when they fall due

■ The cost of raising finance (eg through share capital, loans and other means) to keep the organisation solvent.

Legal compliance

The preparation of financial and payroll information and records is subject to complex legal and regulatory requirements.

It is yet another important role of the accounting and payroll functions to ensure that all legal and regulatory requirements are met. This helps the organisation:

■ To benefit from a *positive reputation and track record* of financial integrity and legal compliance (which may, in turn, enable the organisation to attract and retain investors, customers, suppliers and high quality staff)

■ To *avoid or minimise liabilities* arising from non-compliance, including: financial penalties (in the form of fines) or even imprisonment; the cost of remedial work to bring records and returns into compliance; the loss of shareholder, share market and regulator confidence; and the burden of, more onerous scrutiny in future.

For your assessment, you won't be required to demonstrate knowledge of specific legislation. However, you will be expected to demonstrate an awareness that payroll and accounting staff are *always* required to follow the rules and procedures laid down by their organisation to ensure that working practices comply with legislative and regulatory requirements.

In order to ensure compliance, the organisation should:

■ Make all employees aware of the importance of compliance

■ Brief all employees on their roles and responsibilities under the law (and up date the briefings as the law changes), from the induction of new recruits onwards

■ Base organisational policies and procedures (and related employee training) on legal requirements

■ Put in place checks and controls, to monitor and ensure compliance.

HOW IT WORKS

Southfield Electronics is a supplier of a wide range of consumer electronics appliances to specialist retailers and department stores.

The accounting function regularly supplies the Sales department with information including:

- Breakdowns of sales revenue by region – so that plans can be made to increase sales effort in under-performing regions (and reward the best-performing sales teams)

- Reports on the value of the inventory (stock) of goods held in the warehouse

- Reports on sales revenue to date (compared with budget) and cost of sales activity to date (compared with budget)

- Reports on the amounts owing by each retail customer, and when they fall due, highlighting overdue amounts.

The accounting function supplies the Purchasing department with:

- Reports on expenditure to date (compared with budget) on bought-in materials and services for the organisation

- A list of discrepancies between supplier invoices and purchase orders – so that Purchasing can query this with suppliers.

Recent information has highlighted two issues of concern.

First, there is too much inventory (stock) of some product lines in the warehouse. The value of this inventory is falling due to deterioration and developments in consumer electronics. The Sales and Production managers have been alerted to the need *either* to 'push' the slow-moving product lines harder to customers *or* to adjust production plans to produce fewer items.

Meanwhile, cash flow summaries have highlighted another problem. The Purchasing department accepts 30-day credit terms from suppliers, and insists that they be paid strictly on time. However, the Sales department is giving customers 60 days' credit, and is reluctant to press them for payment. Southfield Electronics is giving money out more readily than it is getting money in – reducing its working capital and creating a threat to its solvency, since its cash reserves are small. The Accounts manager decides to call a meeting to discuss the need for longer credit terms with suppliers *and* stricter credit control with customers.

Task 2

As an accounts clerk at Southfield Electronics, you have been asked by the Chief Accountant to send a brief email to the Sales Manager, Hailey Skommett, notifying her of the cash flow situation, explaining its relevance to the Sales department, and inviting her to submit possible dates/times for a meeting with the Accounts Manager and Production Manager.

Emails at Southfield Electronics appear as follows:

EMAIL

To: hskommett@southfield.co.uk
From: yourname@southfield.co.uk
Date: *[today's date]*
Subject:

Draft the brief email.

THE LEGAL FRAMEWORK

Organisations operate within a framework of laws which is very broad in scope, and deals with a range of specific issues. While you don't have to know about specific legislation in detail for this Unit, you are expected to appreciate the *importance* of an organisation's compliance with the law of the land or region in which it operates.

Compliance with all areas of the law is important because:

- The law is there to protect people from loss and suffering, and ensure minimum acceptable standards of management

- There may be financial penalties (eg fines, compensation) and operational penalties (eg loss of licence) for non-compliance

- Non-compliance can damage the reputation of the organisation, and its ability to attract investors, customers and staff

- Non-compliance can lead to burdens and costs of corrective action, closer scrutiny in future and so on.

For an organisation in the UK, the main sources of law are UK statutes (or Acts of Parliament), EU Directives issued by the European Union, and regulations made under those laws.

It is the responsibility of every member of an organisation to comply with legislation (where you could reasonably be expected to be aware of provisions, as relevant to your job role) – and to monitor and ensure compliance within the area of your responsibility. For example, you have a personal duty not to discriminate against others; not to misuse personal data held on file; not to break health and safety rules; not to engage in criminal activities such as theft or assault at work – and to take appropriate steps if you see anyone else doing so.

As a member of an accounting or payroll function, you also have a shared duty to support the organisation's compliance with requirements for financial controls, records and reports.

The following are some examples of areas regulated under UK and EU law – many of which will have their equivalents in the legal regimes of other parts of the world.

Area of the law	Examples
How the organisation does business	*Contract law*: what constitutes a valid contract, and how rights and obligations under a contract can be enforced
	Data protection and confidentiality: what personal data organisations can legitimately hold and use, to protect the privacy of individuals
	Intellectual property: protecting the rights of the originators of product designs, written texts and artistic works, by preventing their copying and exploitation by others
How the organisation treats its employees	*Employment protection*: protecting employees from unfair dismissal and redundancy practices
	Health and safety: protection of employees and visitors in the workplace
	Working conditions, pay and benefits: minimum standards for remuneration, working hours and so on
	Diversity and equal opportunity: protection against harassment and discrimination at work on the grounds of sex, sexual orientation, race, religion, age or disability
Responsibilities to shareholders/stakeholders (Company law and corporate governance)	Duties of directors of the company
	Keeping accounts and registers
	Preparing and auditing financial statements
	Preparing and circulating annual reports and accounts
Responsibilities to the State	Collection and payment of taxes including VAT to HM Revenue & Customs (HMRC)
	Compilation and provision of reports and returns

Regulatory control

In addition to legislation, there has been an increase in the guidance, monitoring and control of organisational practices through 'watchdog' bodies, voluntary Codes of Practice and industry standards.

- Regulatory bodies oversee the activities of businesses in various areas: examples include the Accounting Standards Board (ASB) and the Health and Safety Executive.

- Codes of Practice may be agreed by industry representative or advisory bodies. For example, there are standards covering the reporting of financial performance and the verification of reports by auditors (Financial Reporting Standards).

- Professional bodies (like the chartered accountancy bodies and the AAT) develop and enforce standards of competence, ethical conduct and continuing professional education in their members.

CHAPTER OVERVIEW

- An organisation pursues a wide range of activities in pursuit of its objectives, and these activities are generally grouped as specialist 'functions'.

- Line functions (such as production and sales) directly further the primary activities of the business, while staff functions (such as accounting and finance) support them by providing resources, policies and information.

- The financial functions in an organisation include financial accounting, management accounting and payroll.

- Their main role is to support managers and staff in other functions by preparing and providing complete, accurate and timely information on the financial implications of their activities (including employing people).

- By providing this information, people in financial roles make an important contribution to the smooth running and efficiency of the business (by supporting planning, control and decision-making); the solvency of the business (by managing working capital, highlighting the cash flow implications of activity, and providing information about debts and the availability of funds to cover them); and the legal compliance of the business (in areas such as financial controls, records and statements).

- Accounting and payroll staff are always required to follow the rules and procedures laid down by their organisation to ensure that legislative and regulatory requirements are complied with.

- Legal compliance embraces not just accounting and payroll practices, but the conduct of the organisation and its employees, in areas such as data protection, health and safety at work, employment protection, equal opportunities and corporate governance.

Keywords

Line functions – activities or departments, such as production and sales, which directly further organisational objectives

Staff functions – activities or departments, such as accounting and finance, HR and IT, which support line functions in their objectives

Financial accounting – activities mainly concerned with the processing and recording of transactions and the production of financial statements for users outside the business

Management accounting – providing financial information to support management decision-making

Cash flow – amounts of cash flowing into and out of the organisation

Working capital – day-to-day finance required for operational activities

Solvency – the ability of the organisation to pay its debts when they fall due

Planning – using information about availability, costs and benefits of resources in order to make decisions about what will be done to achieve the organisation's objectives

Control – using information about activities that have taken place in order to hold managers accountable for those activities and to make decisions about how future activities should take place

Efficiency – achieving objectives with the minimum amount (and minimum waste) of resources

TEST YOUR LEARNING

Test 1

Explain what is meant by a staff function, and give three examples.

Test 2

Explain the differences between financial accounting and management accounting.

Test 3

You have been asked to draft a job description for a Payroll Assistant. Make a list of the typical tasks involved in payroll.

Test 4

Susan, a manager, has been provided with a payroll report she requested from the payroll function. She wanted the report in order to process the wages payments at the end of the month but she also needed it to assess whether sufficient funds in the business current account were available to ensure the payments went through without incurring bank charges.

Bill, the payroll clerk, knew the manager wanted the report so he took a very long time putting it together making sure all the information needed was included and everything on the report was absolutely correct. However due to his careful approach the report has only just been passed to Susan and there is only one day left before the scheduled date for the wages payments.

Evaluate the quality of the payroll information provided in the scenario above.

Test 5

State what you understand by the term 'efficiency', and explain how information provided by an accounting function can help another department to become more efficient.

Test 6

Explain how the information provided by the accounting function can help the organisation to maintain its solvency.

Test 7

Draft a notice for the accounting function's notice board, reminding staff why it is important to comply with all relevant legislation and regulations applicable to their work.

Test 8

As an accounts assistant at Smith's Cleaning Company, you have recently noticed some 'short cuts' being taken in the recording of transactions, and have spoken to your manager (Sue Hahn) about this. She asks you to put in writing, in a memo, some points on how the company can improve its compliance with legal requirements, for an accounting function meeting. In your memo, give four examples of laws which must be complied with in an accounting environment, in addition to regulations on the preparation of financial records and statements.

The company's standard memo form is as follows:

SMITH'S CLEANING COMPANY
MEMORANDUM
To: **From:** **Date:** **Subject**

chapter 3:
THE ORGANISATIONAL FRAMEWORK

chapter coverage 📖

This chapter looks at the organisational framework for working effectively in accounting and finance roles, including reporting structures and various organisational policies and procedures that may apply to your work.

It explains how to use an organisation chart: in the assessment you will use the organisation chart provided to identify who your work colleagues are and to determine chains of command and reporting lines. You may need to refer to the information on policies and procedures when carrying out the tasks in your assessment.

The topics covered are:

✍ Organisation structure

✍ Identifying reporting lines

✍ Organisational policies and procedures

ORGANISATION STRUCTURE

ORGANISATION STRUCTURE is the 'shape' of an organisation, which reflects a number of decisions about how it will function most efficiently, including:

- How the organisation's tasks are grouped and divided to form different *units*, such as functions, departments and sections. This may be done on the basis of function (marketing, production, finance), geography (eg countries or sales territories) or product types.

- How *power, authority and responsibility* are allocated to different levels and positions in the organisation. This creates a hierarchy or CHAIN OF COMMAND, whereby authority flows 'down the line' from senior management to each level of the organisation – and accountability and reports flow back up.

- How different units, tiers and positions in the organisation are linked by *lines of communication and co-operation* – so that their plans and activities can be co-ordinated towards the achievement of overall objectives, and so that individuals and teams receive the information and resources they require to play their part.

Organisation charts

ORGANISATION CHARTS are often used to illustrate the formal structure of an organisation or function. In their most basic form, they use boxed or unboxed *captions* to indicate particular units (eg the Accounting Function) or positions (eg Accounts Manager) and *linking lines* to indicate the relationships and communication between them.

Vertical lines link different tiers or levels, illustrating chains of command (downwards) and reporting lines (upwards).

- Instructions, orders and work requests flow down the chain of command from people with more authority (superiors) to those with less authority (subordinates).

- Reports flow back up the line – because subordinates are ACCOUNTABLE to superiors for the tasks they have been given. Queries may also flow back up the line, if subordinates need to seek or confirm instructions. Certain decisions may have to be 'referred' back up the line if subordinates lack the authority to handle them themselves.

- Your LINE MANAGER is your immediate superior, following the vertical line of command: this is the person directly responsible for requesting work from you and to whom you report directly.

Horizontal lines link units/positions at the same level of the organisation, which are grouped together under the 'umbrella' of the next level up. Units/positions linked in this way need to communicate and co-ordinate their work to meet their shared objectives. They may occasionally be required to work together in CROSS-FUNCTIONAL TEAMS for projects requiring special co-ordination.

A horizontal line joining a vertical line from the side is often used to show 'staff' relationships, where a unit or position doesn't have direct *authority* 'over' the next tier down – but exercises *influence* by giving expert advice, or developing and enforcing policies or procedures, in relevant areas of work.

An IT department may exercise influence over other departments' IT systems development and data security procedures, say – while an accounts department may impose policies for budgeting, invoicing, payment authorisations, expenses claims and so on.

HOW IT WORKS

The organisation chart for Southfield Electrical is as follows, showing how the finance function fits into the overall scheme of things at the firm.

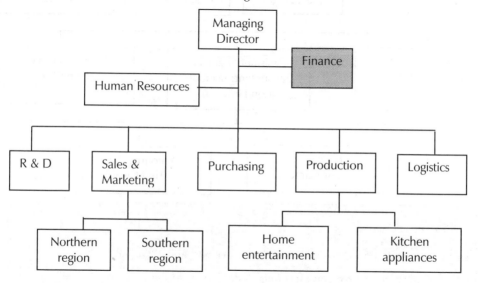

The chart for the finance function is as follows.

Task 1

From the organisation charts shown in 'How it Works' above, identify:

(a)   How many people you (Accounts clerk) directly report to

(b)   Who you would ask if you don't know what to do with a memo about a staff member's National Insurance contributions

(c)   Which three members of the financial accounts department have the same amount of authority

(d)   What difficulties might be caused for you by these members having the same amount of authority

(e)   Who you might appeal to if these difficulties were too much for you

(f)   How a member of the R & D function should issue instructions to a member of the Kitchen Appliances production team

(g)   Whether the finance function has 'line' or 'staff' authority to impose a credit control policy in the logistics department

Document and information flows

The organisation structure affects the accounting system, and the role of the accounting and payroll functions, in terms of:

- how information is collected, and by whom;

- how information is sent up and down the organisation chain, and across the boundaries between different functions; and

- how information should be processed and presented, to suit the needs of different users.

IDENTIFYING REPORTING LINES

When you work within an organisation you are not working in isolation. As we have just seen, you may have colleagues or peers at the same level, managers of varying levels of seniority, and possibly more junior employees to whom you can delegate tasks.

Your job or role description often sets out the reporting and REPORTING PROCEDURE for that role. For whom are you doing tasks? Who needs particular data or documents next? To whom are you accountable for performing a task correctly? To whom should you refer questions and problems?

Reporting lines and procedures will differ from organisation to organisation, depending on the formal structure of the business. In a very small business, for example, all employees may report directly to the owner of the business. In a large multinational company, there could be complex organisational structures for the business as a whole, and each country, site or department within it.

Identifying reporting lines for a given job and task

You are most likely to report on a day-to-day basis to a *designated* supervisor or LINE MANAGER such as the head of your department or section. A line manager is someone who has direct authority over people and activities, down the vertical 'line' of command in the organisation chart. In an accounts department, this is likely to be an accountant or financial controller, or it could be the general office or administration manager.

If you are temporarily working on a particular project, you may report to the PROJECT MANAGER on tasks relating to that specific project. An example might be if you were preparing costings for a new product launch, say, or checking supplier invoices for the installation of a new IT system: such activities may well be organised as a distinct project, with a designated project manager overseeing the work.

You may also find that, on occasion, you are required to do a one-off job for someone to whom you do not normally report. For example, the sales manager may have requested a breakdown of sales by geographical area: in this case, you may report directly to the sales manager on this specific task (by agreement with your line manager).

Organisational policies and procedures may suggest other reporting lines. For example, if you identify a health or safety risk in your work place, the 'appropriate person' to report it to may be the Health and Safety officer or Fire officer.

It is important for you to know to whom you should report both on routine and non-routine matters. For routine tasks, this will most often be your immediate superior, project manager or the person who has asked you to perform a task.

In cases where a matter has to be referred 'above the head' of your immediate superior(s) for decision, you should simply follow the vertical line of command up to the *next highest person*. An example might be where you cannot resolve a conflict with an immediate superior: if she has asked you to do something inappropriate or unethical, say, or has treated you unfairly.

HOW IT WORKS

At Southfield Electronics, there are two accounts clerks – yourself and Amy Laval – employed as a 'shared resource' for two assistant financial accountants and a payroll manager.

Your role includes fulfilling work requests given to you by all three of these individuals, and giving clerical support, as required, to the work of the financial accounts section as a whole.

One day:

- You are struggling to complete a piece of work given to you by Ron Howard, which appears to contain incomplete information.

- You have just finished a batch of payslips, which need checking.

- You have just received a delivery of stationery supplies for the section, but before signing the receipt note, you notice that the delivery does not seem to be complete, according to the copy of the purchase order sent to you by the purchasing department.

- Both Kellie McDonald and Ron Howard have given you urgent tasks to perform the following day, and you know you will not have time to do both of them. You have spoken to both Kellie and Ron about this – but neither of them will back down: they each think their work is most important.

What are the appropriate reporting and referral lines in this situation?

- Your queries about the first task should be referred to Ron Howard, because he was the one who gave you the task.

- The payslips should be given to Jane Chu (the Payroll manager) for checking, because this is the work area for which she is responsible.

- The query about the stationery order should be referred to the purchasing department, since they are responsible for the purchase order, and dealing with suppliers.

- If Kellie and Ron cannot come to agreement, you may have to refer the matter to *their* superior, who has the authority to decide whose work has priority.

Task 2

You are employed in the accounts department and have been asked to compile some costings for training requests submitted by accounts department members. To whom might you report on matters relating to this task?

ORGANISATIONAL POLICIES AND PROCEDURES

Organisational policies and procedures will influence most aspects of your everyday working practice, both in technical matters (ie how accounting and information-processing tasks should be carried out) and in regard to your behaviour in the workplace (including areas such as health, safety and security, timekeeping, dress, confidentiality of information, recycling and other 'green' practices – and so on).

A POLICY is a statement of how an organisation wants and expects activities to be carried out. They provide strong guidelines for action, decision-making and problem-solving. Equal opportunities policies, for example, are statements of the organisation's attitude to eliminating discrimination in the workplace, and how this should be done in selecting people for jobs, training, rewards and promotions.

A PROCEDURE is a standard sequence of steps or operations necessary to perform an activity. An organisation will have formal or informal procedures relating to a wide range of matters such as: the handling of cash receipts, the recording of payroll details, the processing of expenses claims, the authorisation of payments and the secure storage of data.

Why is it important to adhere to policy and procedure?

Often, policies and procedures are regarded as routine – or even as a nuisance, if there are more convenient 'short cuts' in performing a task. However, it is important to adhere to formal organisation requirements – and to know *why* you are doing so.

Policies and procedures are put in place to:

- *Support efficiency.* They enable people to perform routine, repetitive or foreseeable tasks correctly, without having to waste time and resources analysing and planning them afresh every time: in other words, you don't have to 'reinvent the wheel'.

- *Support compliance.* They generally build in the requirements of law and regulation, ensuring minimum standards of practice (and possibly 'good' practice).

- *Protect people.* Health, safety and security policies and procedures, for example, are put in place to protect you, others working around you and people visiting your workplace.

- *Protect finance, property, information and other assets of the organisation.* Financial control procedures, for example, are established to minimise temptations and opportunities for fraud and mismanagement of resources.

Procedures may also incorporate *rules*. If a policy is 'the way it should be done', and a procedure is 'the way it is done', a rule is 'the way it *must* be done (in order to be done correctly)'. Examples of rules include: maintaining the confidentiality of financial information; seeking required authorisations for transactions; and keeping fire doors clear and closed.

Let's look briefly at some of the organisational policies and procedures that are most likely to affect your work in an accounting or payroll environment.

Health and safety

Most policies and procedures for health and safety in the workplace are based on provisions set out in law such as the Health and Safety at Work Act 1974 and related regulations.

Health and safety at work is about the prevention of accidents and ill-health caused by working conditions and work practices.

All organisations with five or more employees must have a written Health and Safety Policy, continually updated and circulated to all employees. As an employee, you have a duty to study this document: you will normally be asked to sign a form stating that you have read it and are willing to take responsibility (in relevant areas) for complying with the policy.

Specific occupational health and safety policies may cover a range of issues such as: the duty of all employees and managers to contribute to a healthy and safe work environment; the use of safety measures and equipment, where required; non-smoking; the participation of staff in regular fire and evacuation drills; and the reporting of risks and accidents to appropriate officials (eg a Health and Safety or Fire officer).

There should be detailed *procedures* for operations such as: the use of fire alarms and equipment; the evacuation of the premises in the event of fire or other threats; the labelling, storage and handling of potentially dangerous workplace chemicals; the safe use and maintenance of electrical equipment and dangerous tools; the reporting of identified health and safety hazards; and the recording of accidents (eg in an accident book).

HOW IT WORKS

Southfield Electronics has a range of policies and procedures, which are published in Procedures Manuals for each function and work site, and also posted on the corporate intranet for employees to consult on their computer terminals.

Its Evacuation Procedure, for example, appears as follows.

EVACUATION OF THE PREMISES IN THE EVENT OF EMERGENCY

In the event of an emergency such as fire or terrorist threat all employees are required to leave the building by the designated route as quickly as possible. They are advised to remain calm and not to linger to gather personal belongings.

Employees are advised not to use the lifts in the event of a fire emergency, as lifts may cease to operate at any time. Particular attention should be paid to evacuees who have special needs (for example, those in wheelchairs or with impaired sight or hearing), and members of staff should help them out.

Once they have left the building, employees and visitors should go immediately to the designated Assembly Point and ensure that any visitors or others on the premises at the time of evacuation, who do not know where to go, are directed and assisted to the Assembly Point by members of staff.

Employees should wait at the Assembly Point. The Safety Officer will carry a roster of everyone signed in as being in the building, and will 'call a roll' at the Assembly Point. Each person should respond when their name is called.

No-one is permitted to return to the building until instructed to do so by a senior official or the Safety Officer.

Task 3

You are the accounts clerk at Southfield Electronics, and you have noticed that several members of the accounts department have been taking the lifts, or even staying in the offices, during fire evacuation drills. You have a word with your supervisor about this, and she refers you to the Safety Officer – who asks you to perform the following tasks, with your supervisor's permission.

(a)   Re-draft the Evacuation Procedure as a poster for the accounts department, setting out more clearly what members should do.

(b)   Add a short paragraph, explaining the importance of complying with the procedure during drills.

Security

Security policies and procedures are designed to protect the physical security of assets (such as computers or petty cash); the physical security of employees (eg from attack or intimidation); and the security of information (eg from unauthorised access, theft or tampering).

Security measures in an office environment can range from simple rules about locking doors, windows, filing cabinets and petty cash boxes at the end of the day – to more complex procedures for:

- Controlling access to areas of a building (eg using security doors, sign-in procedures and identity badges or security cards)

- Controlling access to the computer system (eg using passwords and authorisation codes)

- Training staff to handle potentially unsafe situations, and to report unidentified strangers and intruders in the office.

Working hours and time-keeping

Policies will generally be laid out in regard to issues such as: working hours, office opening hours, the taking of lunch breaks (and holiday entitlements), time-keeping and punctuality. There may be detailed procedures for clocking on and off, filling out time sheets, operating flexi-time schemes and other forms of flexible working – and so on.

Such issues are important for:

- The efficiency of the organisation, ensuring that it can plan for adequate staffing – and rely on those plans, once made

- Fraud prevention, ensuring that people work the hours they are paid for

- Effective working relations, ensuring people honour their commitments to the team and 'pull their weight'

- Individual wellbeing, ensuring some 'work-life balance' – which also supports long-term productivity

- Individual work planning and scheduling, ensuring that workloads are planned within the hours available in the day! (We look at this in more detail later in the Workbook.)

Maintenance of your work area

Your personal WORK AREA may include your desk, the area around your desk, and other areas of the office in which you regularly move and work.

Your immediate work area will often be your own responsibility, in general terms. It will, to some degree, define you to your colleagues – and external visitors. If your desk is tidy and documents are filed way, this gives an impression of a tidy mind and an efficient employee. Conversely, an untidy work area may create the impression of someone who does not care about their work. A tidy and organised work area also ensures that you – and others around you – can work effectively and efficiently: we look further at this later in the Workbook.

There may be departmental rules or guidelines as to how your work area should be organised and maintained, mainly aimed at ensuring that offices maintain a professional image, and reflect the corporate image of the organisation, particularly in areas which are visited by outsiders.

Organisations often have rules regarding *personal effects* displayed in work areas, such as photographs of family and friends, posters or postcards. This will often depend upon the type of environment in which you work. In a large open plan office which rarely receives visits from external parties such as customers, suppliers or the general public, it might be quite acceptable to have family photographs or amusing cartoons displayed (providing that they do not offend those working around you).

However, in an office regularly visited by customers, the desire to convey professionalism may lead to organisational restrictions on the type or number of personal possessions allowed in the workplace.

Even if there are no formal 'rules' regarding such matters, there may be informal 'understandings'. Ask colleagues or your supervisor, or observe the work areas of your colleagues to find out what is appropriate – and watch out for similar hints in the assessment case study.

Another important aspect of this is that tidiness supports *data security*. You will generally be expected to tidy away confidential documents once they are finished with, or likely to be left unattended. However, in some organisations, there may be an explicit CLEAR DESK POLICY, which requires that everything must be cleared from your desktop at the end of each day, in order to ensure disciplined work practices and to reduce the vulnerability of data to theft and espionage.

Confidentiality of information

In an accounting role, you will come across a variety of confidential information – and you must be extremely careful how you deal with it. As we saw earlier in this chapter, you have a key role in co-ordinating flows of financial information in the organisation. But what information should 'flow' – and to whom? What is 'confidential' information?

Some information (in files, reports, emails or letters, say) may be clearly marked as being 'confidential' (or 'private', or 'limited access' or 'for authorised individuals only').

Certain types of information may be designated as confidential by law, organisational policy and professional codes of practice.

- Details of customers and suppliers must not be disclosed to anyone outside the organisation.

- Personal data about employees, for example payroll details, must be kept strictly confidential, to protect privacy.

- Financial information is likely to be highly sensitive – but there are other categories of information which, if disclosed, could be used for purposes harmful to the organisation or its personnel: there are likely to be strict rules about the disclosure of security procedures and codes, details of legal proceedings, new product plans and so on.

Look out for any such information in the assessment case study, as well as any explicit policies about CONFIDENTIALITY.

HOW IT WORKS

At Southfield Electrical, the Sales Manager has forwarded to the Financial Accountant a letter from an estate agent, requesting financial information about one of the firm's major customers, which is applying to rent a commercial property. The information is needed as soon as possible, by fax or email, in order to secure approval for the rental. The Sales Manager has asked the accounts department to help.

Is there a confidentiality issue here? Yes, there is. The Financial Accountant would certainly need the customer's permission to disclose any information. Since the request seems inappropriate, she should also confirm the identity of the person making the request. If everything is above board, there is still a confidentiality issue in how the information is sent: fax can be easily intercepted (and so can e-mail). The information should be sent securely, and clearly marked 'private and confidential'.

Task 4

How would you deal with each of the following requests, and why?

(a)   A customer asks for the address and telephone number of another customer

(b)   A colleague asks you for the home address of two other employees, knowing that you have access to this data via payroll records

(c)   The company's security guard asks for the names of the visitors expected by your department that week

Secure storage of data and information

Information held in files, records and computers needs to be protected from accidental or malicious damage, loss, theft, sabotage, interference – and prying eyes. Interference may just be casual – someone playing around with your terminal when you are not there – but it can still result in damage, disruption or loss of data. Potential threats to data security include computer viruses, hacking or 'phishing', systems failure and corruption/loss of data.

It is especially important to keep accounting data secure, because it is needed to run the business properly; it is often commercially sensitive; and (as in the case of personnel and payroll data) it may be private, confidential and protected by privacy and data protection laws.

There will almost certainly be policies and procedures covering data security aspects such as:

- The non-removal of data and equipment from the premises

- The frequent backing-up of computerised data, and the storage of backups separately from the original data, so that there are safe copies in case of systems failure, data corruption or fire

- The use of anti-virus software, firewalls and other protective tools on all computers, to prevent malicious corruption and theft of data

- The use of passwords to prevent unauthorised users from gaining access to computer systems or files (often with additional policies regarding the complexity and regular change of passwords)

- The use of authorisations to control access to security-coded paper-based files

- The non-divulging of passwords, security codes and other data security measures to other parties.

Document retention

There will be additional policies and procedures for *document retention:* the period that documents need to be kept on file. There are legal obligations to keep certain financial documents for prescribed lengths of time.

- Many accounting and banking records (including ledgers, invoices, cheques and bills of exchange, paying-in counterfoils, bank statements and instructions to banks) should be kept for six years.

- Employee records (including staff personnel records, time cards and piecework records, payroll records and expenses claims) should also be kept for six years – and accident report books, permanently!

If in doubt, you should consult organisational policy documents, or your supervisor, to check on what these are – and look out for any specific policy information set out in the assessment case study.

Departmental deadlines

Some activities of financial functions are bound by strict deadlines, and these should be clearly incorporated in relevant plans and procedures.

Payroll preparation is one example. If an employee is to be paid on the 30th of the month, the pay must be in his/her bank account on that date. Any changes to pay rates must be included on the first available payroll. Tax deductions have to be paid over to HM Revenue and Customs by a due date: if payment is delayed, the employer may have to pay interest. Similarly, other deductions, such as pension contributions, need to be paid over to third parties regularly and on time, otherwise the employee's entitlements could be affected.

In financial accounting, there are strict, externally imposed deadlines for the preparation and lodging of statutory financial statements and reports (eg the year-end lodgement date). These, in turn, impose internal deadlines for the gathering and processing of information, auditing and so on.

However, as we will see in later chapters, it is very important to meet *any* agreed departmental or team deadline for the completion of work, because your work impacts on the work of others.

HOW IT WORKS

One of your tasks at Southfield Electronics is to list any cheques received in the post each morning. This listing is then passed on to the cashier, James Thorne, for entry into the cash receipts book and updating of the sales ledger (receivables ledger). He can only carry out his daily task once you have finished yours.

If you do not finish the cheque listing early in the morning (because you have not planned your work routine) or if you mislay the cheque listing for the day (because your work area is untidy or your files disordered), this will impact on James' work for the day as well as yours.

Authorisation procedures

Many accounting and payroll tasks require authorisations, as part of the organisation's system of financial controls to prevent fraud and mismanagement of resources. An authorisation is a point in a procedure at which confirmation or permission to proceed must be obtained from an individual with appropriate authority.

In payroll, for example:

- All *variations* to the payroll must be properly authorised, including temporary variations such as overtime. Permanent variations, such as salary increases, will usually be authorised by *senior managers* and it is likely that you will be familiar with their signatures. However, overtime is likely to be authorised by line managers. The employee's record or contract of employment will let you know if (s)he is entitled to overtime payments – but how do you know if the actual overtime figure has been correctly authorised?

- Most large organisations will have a *list of AUTHORISED SIGNATORIES* for each department. This is a list of people authorised to approve changes to the payroll, together with a *specimen signature*. The list should also indicate whether the person can authorise permanent and/or temporary changes, to what value, for what department, and to what grades of employee. If you are a payroll clerk, you will need a copy of this list so that you can check that variations are correctly authorised!

- If variations are *not* correctly authorised, you will need to bring this to your supervisor's or line manager's attention. (Do not assume that it is an innocent mistake: the employee could be trying to obtain an increased salary or overtime payments fraudulently...)

Similar policies and procedures (involving authorisations and designated signatories) will invariably be in place for operations such as:

- The issuing of purchase orders
- The preparation of cheques and other payments
- The processing of expense claims
- The processing of petty cash.

These policies may vary from organisation to organisation, but the principles will be similar.

Task 5

What information will you need to know, and check, to ensure that authorisations comply with procedure?

You should be informed of the specific policies and procedures applicable to your work role, via policy documents and procedure manuals (and their online equivalents) and/or by induction, training and coaching within your department.

In your assessment, you should be given a copy of any specific policies of the case study organisation which you are expected to apply (in a simulated accounting or payroll task) or use (eg by summarising them and/or explaining their importance to others).

The most important point is that individuals working in financial roles need to:

- Find out what the applicable policies and procedures are

- Ensure that they understand the requirements (or seek help to understand them)

- Ensure that they follow or adhere to the requirements, in all relevant situations.

HOW IT WORKS

Southfield Electronics has a policy about authorising expenditure.

Ian Hamilton, an employee in the Sales department, has been asked to organise the office Christmas party. He has booked caterers for the event, but they require a deposit of £150.

Ian must fill in a cheque requisition form, giving details of the payment, and attach a VAT invoice or receipt as evidence of the payment. Ian doesn't have such documentation, so just puts 'None' in the space on the cheque requisition form.

The form is sent to the Sales supervisor for authorisation. However, she knows that for amounts between £100 and £500, requisitions must be authorised by a department manager. The form is therefore forwarded to the Sales manager – who signs it, and sends it to the Financial Accounts department.

Jenny Faulkner calls the Sales manager to point out that the requisition should not have been authorised, and cannot be processed, in the absence of evidence of payment. The requisition form will be returned to Ian. Jenny advises that Ian, or the Sales manager, can pay the deposit himself – and then fill out a cheque requisition for reimbursement, attaching the VAT receipt for the expense. However, they will have to bear in mind that correctly completed and authorised cheque requisition forms must be with the accounts department by 10 am to guarantee that a cheque is prepared on the same day.

Meanwhile, the company also has a written agreement with its bank regarding who is allowed to sign the organisation's cheques. The bank will only accept cheques that have been signed by the authorised signatories. For cheques up to a value of £8,000, the signature of a director is required. Cheques for *more* than this amount require the signatures of two directors.

Task 6

Following the 'How It Works' scenario above, Jenny Faulkner asks you, the Accounts clerk, to send an email to all departments, reminding them of the requirements of the cheque requisition policy, and reminding them of the consequences of failing to adhere to the policy.

Southfield's email software looks as follows.

EMAIL

To:	allstaff@southfield.co.uk
From:	yname@southfield.co.uk
Date:	[Today's date]
Subject:	

Draft the text of the email.

CHAPTER OVERVIEW

- Organisation structure reflects the grouping of tasks into units and functions; the flow of authority and responsibility; and lines of communication and co-operation between individuals and units. This can be depicted in organisation charts.

- The organisation structure partly determines reporting lines, in establishing a 'chain of command'. Your designated supervisor or line manager is your direct superior in this chain, to whom you report most directly.

- Reporting lines and relationships are also based on: who asked you to perform a given task; who is the manager of the project to which the task contributes; and who is the most appropriate person to deal with a given matter. Some matters may need to be 'referred upwards' to a superior manager.

- Organisational policies and procedures will influence most aspects of your everyday working practice. It is important to adhere to them, to support efficiency and compliance – and to protect people and assets.

- Some key examples of policies and procedures in an accounting environment include: health and safety; security; working hours and timekeeping; maintenance of your work area; confidentiality of information; secure storage of data and information; document retention; adherence to departmental deadlines; authorisations and designated signatories.

Keywords

Organisation structure – the 'shape' of an organisation, made up of defined units, levels of authority and communication lines

Chain of command – the line down which authority flows in the organisation structure

Organisation charts – diagrams depicting the formal structure of an organisation

Accountable – the duty of a subordinate to report to a superior on the outcome of the tasks (s)he has been given

Line manager – your immediate superior in the line or chain of command

Cross-functional teams – teams which include members from different functions in the organisation, for the purpose of co-ordination (eg in carrying out projects)

Reporting procedure – the channels through which an employee reports to a superior official

Project manager – the manager appointed to run a particular project

Policy – a statement of how an organisation wants and expects activities to be carried out

Procedure – a standard sequence of steps necessary to perform an activity

Work area – your desk, chair, surrounding furniture and space

Clear desk policy – an organisational policy that all desks must be left clear at the end of each working day

Confidentiality – the duty not to disclose restricted, private or otherwise sensitive information to unauthorised parties

Authorised signatories – people who are authorised to sign the organisation's cheques and to authorise other operations

TEST YOUR LEARNING

Test 1

Explain what is meant by the 'chain of command' and how you can use this to determine who your line manager is.

Test 2

Give examples of the types of communication that flow (a) down and (b) up the organisation structure.

Test 3

You have been asked to prepare a 'To Do List' for the Accounts department, in relation to the relocation of the company's offices. This is being managed as a cross-functional project by the Office manager. Because of the pressure of work from the Accounts supervisor, you are not sure you will be able to complete the 'To Do List' in the time given to you. Who should you report to about this?

Test 4

Explain why it is important to adhere to office policies and procedures.

Test 5

Most employees like to personalise their work area with personal objects. Explain how appropriate this may or may not be in:

(a) An Accounts department where there are rarely any visits from non-employees; and

(b) A reception area which is open to the public.

Test 6

Describe four policies that can help to keep computerised accounting data secure.

Test 7

How would you respond to the following information requests?

(a) Your supervisor asks you for details of the latest R & D expenditure on new products

(b) A telephone caller, saying she is a financial journalist, asks you for details of your upcoming plans for new products

(c) A customer calls asking for the bank details of one of your fellow employees, stating that the customer wishes to pay a cheque into her bank account. You can find this information from the payroll records

(d) One of the senior accounts assistants has asked you to photocopy the notes for a training course that another rival company uses. You notice that the course notes have the copyright © symbol on them.

Test 8

Explain the meaning of 'authorisations' and 'designated signatories' and why they are important.

chapter 4:
COMMUNICATION SKILLS

— chapter coverage 📖 —

This chapter, together with Chapter 5, will develop the knowledge and skills required to communicate effectively in a range of formats and contexts. Chapter 5 covers the presentation of information in reports, letters, memoranda and emails.

In this chapter, we focus on communicating clearly, using business language, and demonstrating numeracy skills appropriate to your role.

This chapter explains the approach you should take in the assessment in order to write business documents of a sufficiently high standard. It also explains the numeracy skills you may require in the assessment. You should use the tasks within the chapter and the questions at the end to practise and develop your skills.

The topics covered are:

✍ Effective business communication

✍ Message content

✍ Presentation

✍ Business language

✍ Numeracy skills

EFFECTIVE BUSINESS COMMUNICATION

What is business communication?

As we saw in chapter 2, working effectively in accounting and finance is fundamentally about the effective preparation, giving and receiving of information. As we will see in later chapters, it is also about working effectively with other people to achieve shared objectives. All of this means: communication!

COMMUNICATION is, at its most basic, the transmission or exchange of information: putting across a message. However, there are many different purposes for doing this:

- To inform: to give people data they require

- To persuade: to get others to agree to, or do, something

- To request: to ask for something

- To confirm: to check that data is correct and that different parties have the same understanding of it

- To build effective working relationships.

All of these activities underpin efficient working and constructive working relationships.

The communication process

Effective communication is a two-way process, often shown as a 'cycle'. Signals or messages are sent by the communicator and received by the target recipient, who sends back some form of confirmation that the message has been received and understood.

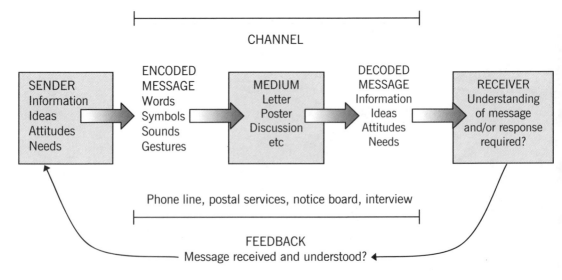

There are some key points to note in this model.

- *Encoding and decoding.* You have to choose the words, symbols, diagrams and numbers you use carefully, so that (a) they accurately convey what you mean and (b) your target audience will be able to *interpret* what you mean correctly.

- *Medium and channel of communication.* Some means of communication are more appropriate and effective than others in a business context. If you get the choice of whether to carry out a communication task using a letter, memo, email, report or informal note – or, in real working life, a telephone call or face-to-face discussion – you will need to consider factors such as: whether speed is important; whether there is the need for written confirmation; which format will best support you in getting your message across to the recipient; and which is the most efficient method in terms of time and cost. This is considered in more detail in Chapter 5.

- *Feedback.* Feedback is the reaction of the audience which indicates whether your message has (or has not) been received and understood. It can range from a smile or frown (in face-to-face communication), to an email giving confirmation or seeking clarification, or a person's taking (or not taking) the action you've requested. It is your responsibility, as communicator, to seek feedback and adjust your message until you're satisfied you've got the result you want.

Task 1

Suggest the most effective medium for communication in the following situations.

(a) New stationery is urgently required from the office goods supplier.

(b) The managing director wants to give a message to all staff.

(c) A member of staff has been absent five times in the past month, and her manager intends to take action.

(d) You need information quickly from another department.

(e) You have to explain a complicated procedure to a group of people.

Communicating effectively, clearly and appropriately

This Unit requires you to demonstrate that you can 'communicate effectively, clearly and appropriately' in a range of work-related tasks. So what makes communication effective, clear and appropriate?

Attribute	Explanation
Using appropriate formats	Selecting the right format (letter, email, memorandum etc) for the job
Observing format conventions and house style	Using formats correctly: observing conventions of structure, format and style, within organisational guidelines and 'house style'
Professionally presented	Ensuring that documents are neat, legible, concise, helpfully structured and smartly presented: showing competence and awareness of business needs
Technically correct	Ensuring that content is accurate, appropriately detailed (for different levels of requirement) and checked for factual/data and typographical errors
Clearly understandable	Tailored to the writer's purpose in communicating (so that a clear message is sent) and to the information needs, language and capabilities of its audience (so that the message can be received)
Projecting the appropriate corporate image	Reflecting a general image of professionalism and competence – including appropriate formality – and the specific desired image or 'character' of the organisation
Achieving its purpose	Obtain feedback to check that the communication has been *effective*. Has it 'done its job'? Has it got the response it aimed for? If not: adjust and try again!

MESSAGE CONTENT

Technically correct

The information you provide, in an accounting role, is likely to be relied on by others, and factual and numerical errors may have serious consequences for their decision-making and results – and for your performance evaluation, credibility and reputation!

This should go without saying, and it is perhaps unlikely that you would *knowingly* give out information that is technically incorrect. However, there is always the possibility of *unknowingly* conveying inaccurate information, or making *careless* errors – and you should be aware of this at all times.

- You may need to verify information, by checking the accuracy of the source, or cross-checking with other sources.

- If you are not confident in your knowledge or competence in a particular area, you may need to check with a more expert colleague, or with your supervisor.

- Always check the assumptions, logical processes and numerical operations (or 'workings') behind a piece of work, before submitting it.

Task 2

Three pieces of work, completed by a colleague in your section, have just been returned with queries, or with requests for the work to be redone. On checking the work, you find both factual and calculation errors. How would you explain to your colleague the importance of ensuring that information is technically correct?

Clear and understandable

It is always the responsibility of the *sender* of a message to ensure that the message has been received and understood: don't expect your target audience to do your work for you!

Take care with the language and terminology you use: tailor it to the *needs and abilities of the person with whom you are communicating*. In some cases you will be giving information to others in the Accounting department who are, like you, familiar with accounting terminology. However, if you are giving information to customers, or to the Marketing department, say, you could not take for granted that your accountancy knowledge will be shared!

Avoid JARGON: technical terms or buzz words that only fellow technicians will know. Think about whether any *diagrams* you use will be meaningful to another person – and add labels and explanatory notes if you think a reader will need help 'decoding' your meaning.

When planning communications, think about your:

- **Purpose**: what do you need to get across? How do you need the other person to respond?

- **Audience**: what language will they understand? What are their needs?

- **Structure and Style**: what format, order, layout and language will be most helpful in achieving your purpose, given your intended audience?

(You might like to remember this as a checklist for message planning, with the helpful mnemonic: PASS!)

HOW IT WORKS

Clare Francis is one of the assistant management accountants at Southfield Electronics. She has received a request from Kate Saltmarsh (the management accountant) and Taylor Smith (a new sales manager) for a summary of the comparison of the monthly sales per product type to budget for November. Both Kate and Taylor have requested the information to be sent via email.

Although Clare is sending the same information to both people, she decides to word the messages slightly differently. Kate is an accountant with detailed knowledge of accounting terminology, whereas it is unlikely that the new sales manager would have such detailed knowledge of the subject. The two emails might look like this.

EMAIL

To:	ksaltmarsh@southfield.co.uk
From:	cfrancis@southfield.co.uk
Date:	8 December 20X8
Subject:	Sales variances – November

In response to your query, the following sales variances by product type were incurred in November:

Product	Variance
MP3 players	£14,300 adverse
Portable DVD players	£2,700 favourable
DVD/VHS combo players	£21,600 adverse
Digital TVs	£18,600 favourable

If you require further detail, let me know.

Clare

EMAIL

To:	tsmith@southfield.co.uk
From:	cfrancis@southfield.co.uk
Date:	8 December 20X8
Subject:	Comparison of actual sales to budgeted sales – November

In response to your query, I have compared the *actual* sales per product type for November to the *budgeted* sales for that product, with the following results:

MP3 players	– sales were £14,300 less than budget
Portable DVD players	– sales were £2,700 more than budget
DVD/VHS combo players	– sales were £21,600 less than budget
Digital TVs	– sales were £18,600 more than budget

Clare

Keep it short and simple!

Here's another helpful mnemonic: KISS! Business people have limited time in which to peruse communications – and that time is worth money to them and their organisations. So business communication, while never abrupt or discourteous, should always be short, to the point, and easy to use. 'Keeping it Short and Simple' may mean:

- Ensuring your message is well structured (eg in clear topic paragraphs)

- Making it easy to read (eg legible and well spaced on the page, and written in reasonably short sentences)

- Being unambiguous (without potential misunderstandings from double-meaning words or vague phrases)

- Avoiding the use of jargon

- Eliminating unnecessary words and phrases

- Separating out detailed data, which would interrupt the flow of your main information or argument. Detail can be placed in appendices or attachments, or summarised in tables or diagrams.

Verbal or visual?

Consider what format will make your information clear, easy to use, professional-looking – and, if you are trying to be persuasive, impactful.

Verbal communication (using words or text) is useful for conveying the thread of an argument, and the meaning of information. However, it can overload readers with limited time to read and absorb. You might like to use visual elements – such as headings and bullet points – to *organise* textual information into more manageable 'chunks', with clear signposts for the reader.

Detailed data may be more clearly organised in a table, or headed columns, to show the reader how it is grouped and classified. Even more visual formats, such as charts, graphs and diagrams, may be used to highlight aspects such as comparisons, correlations and trends. (We look at the use of diagrams in Chapter 5, when we discuss report writing.)

PRESENTATION

Professionalism and corporate image

Written communications may be the first or only contact people have with you in a business situation – and first impressions count! A letter or email is like an 'ambassador' for you, your organisation and your department.

In order to convey professionalism, the presentation of your message should show the following qualities.

- If handwritten, it should be legible (readable), neat and free of excessive visible errors and corrections (such as crossings out or Tippex). Neatness and legibility are the *absolute minimum* requirement in a professional context: do not compromise on this – whether in your work or in your assessment file!

- It should demonstrate competence in using word-processing or email software, and whatever tools you are using (including the use of diagrams).

- It should demonstrate some regard to the needs of the user, such as clear diagram labelling, cross-referencing of appendices, and citing of information sources.

- It may even display some features of good 'design', such as creative use of space, and the use of devices such as <u>underlining</u>, **bold** or *italic* type, for headings and emphasis.

Communications also create or reflect the image that outsiders have of an organisation: its CORPORATE IMAGE. Your organisation may seek to project itself as creative, youthful and informal – or as reliable, mature and traditional. Your communications should reflect that image, and there may be CORPORATE IDENTITY and house style guidelines to help you in doing this. You may, for example, be instructed to include corporate logos; to use specially designed letter, memo or email stationery; to use particular layouts, colours or typefaces; and/or to include certain standard elements (such as blocks of text accompanying your signature at the bottom of letters and emails).

If such guidelines exist – follow them. Look out for any specimen communications in your assessment case study material that suggest what the guidelines might be.

Task 3

What do you think the advantages are of using a computer word-processing package for producing business documents and communications?

BUSINESS LANGUAGE

Formality

Styles of communication range from extremely informal and friendly through to extremely formal and impersonal. It is important that the right style is used in appropriate contexts!

There is the basic requirement that *any* business communication must be courteous, businesslike and professional. This does not necessarily mean 'formal': if you work in an organisation where all levels of employees and managers are on first name terms, the style of communication will tend to be less formal than in an organisation where all managers are addressed by their title and surname, eg as Mr Jones or Ms Smith.

Even in relatively informal settings, however, the appropriate style for business communication will be significantly more formal than you might use in a note, email or text message to a friend. You *must* bear this in mind – both at work and in your assessment!

Formality expresses respect for the position and professionalism of the person you are dealing with, and signals the seriousness with which you take your own work role. Formality is also important in getting your message across, since many people find text-message-style abbreviations and slang terms not just disrespectful and unprofessional – but difficult to decode!

A businesslike formal style is written in full, grammatical sentences, avoiding 'text-message'-style abbreviations, and even abbreviated forms such as 'there's' or 'we've'. (The full form 'there is' or 'we have' are preferable.) Your language should be direct (not ambiguous), accessible (but not clichéd) and factual (not too emotional or 'colourful'): avoid colloquial or slang expressions. You should keep to the point and avoid unnecessary digressions. Your tone should be appropriate for business relationships: not overly 'familiar' or friendly in tone, or personal in content, and referring to people by their title and surname – unless they have expressly invited you to be more informal.

Task 4

You have been asked to coach some junior members of your department on the use of formal business communication. Set out the advice given in the previous paragraph of text, in a more visual and easy to use format, as 'Dos and Don'ts of acceptable business style'.

NUMERACY SKILLS

You should already have been developing your numeracy skills in your studies for other Units, such as *Basic Accounting*. So you won't be starting from scratch in preparing to demonstrate your competence in this assessment!

The important thing here is to recognise when your numeracy skills are being called on, select the right techniques and tools to use – and apply them carefully and accurately.

Addition and subtraction

Addition is used in sub-totalling and totalling amounts: columns of debits and credits, for example, or itemised costs, or the total output of team members, or an amount payable after the addition of VAT.

Subtraction is used for operations such as calculating net pay after deductions, or amounts payable after deduction of a discount.

Addition and subtraction should, with practice, be a fairly straightforward operation (with or without a calculator). However, you do need to think carefully that you are selecting the right items or numbers to add or subtract, from a list of data.

Multiplication and division

Multiplication is used in operations such as calculating annual costs from monthly costs (multiplying by 12), or calculating total costs from unit costs (cost per unit multiplied by the number of units). It is also used when dealing with fractions and percentages 'of' an amount.

Division is used in operations such as calculating the cost 'per' unit (total cost divided by number of units).

Multiplication and division should, similarly, become a fairly straightforward operation with practice (although in this case, a calculator certainly helps!). Again, however, you need to think carefully about whether multiplication or division are required, and which items of data to select for the operation. We will look at some practical examples in a moment.

Fractions

A FRACTION is a ratio of two numbers. ¼ means 'one part in four': it also means 1 *divided by* 4.

To find 'a fraction of' something, you simply use multiplication. Say the cost of 20 invoiced items is £360, but you only ordered and received eight items. You need to work out the cost of eight out of the 20 items.

8/20 × £360 = £144

When working with fractions (especially if you aren't using a calculator), it helps to use the simplest version of the fraction, with the lowest numbers. You can do this by a process called 'cancelling down': simply divide the top and bottom numbers of the fraction by the same amounts, until they won't go any further.

Because fractions are ratios or relationships, they stay the same as long as you multiply or divide the top and the bottom numbers *by the same amount*.

$$\frac{8}{20} = \frac{4}{10} = \frac{2}{5} \qquad \frac{24}{30} = \frac{12}{15} = \frac{4}{5}$$

In these examples, you might like to stop cancelling down at 4/10 – or use equal top-and-bottom multiplication to convert 4/5 into 8/10, because tenths are very easy to work with, and easy to convert into decimal points (8/10 = 0.8) and percentages (8/10 = 80/100 = 80%).

If you are using a calculator, you will need to familiarise yourself with the 'fraction button' (if any) and how it is used.

HOW IT WORKS

You are investigating inaccuracies in the work of the Accounts section at Southfield Electronics. You have been told that three out of every 12 invoices in the section's work contain an error, and you want to calculate how many errors that makes over a whole day's work of 88 invoices.

You could rephrase the problem as follows.

$$\frac{3}{12} = \frac{?}{88} \qquad\qquad \text{Cancelling down:} \qquad \frac{1}{4} = \frac{?}{88}$$

What do you have to multiply 4 by to get to 88? Division is the reverse operation to multiplication, so you work backwards: $88 \div 4 = 22$. Now you know you have to multiply the bottom of the fraction by 22, and in order to keep the ratio the same, you have to do the same to the top.

$$\frac{1 \times 22}{4 \times 22} = \frac{22}{88}$$

If three out of 12 invoices are faulty, then – at the same rate of errors – 22 out of the daily total of 88 invoices may be faulty!

There is another way of thinking about this. You could say that 3/12 or ¼ (one quarter) of all invoices have an error. 3/12 of 88 invoices is calculated as:

$3/12 \times 88 = 22$

So 22 invoices out of 88 will have an error.

Percentages

A PERCENTAGE is a proportion or rate per hundred parts (*per cent*). It is used to express any proportion in relation to a whole: fractions can also be expressed as percentages, by multiplying by 100.

$$\frac{1}{4} \times \frac{100}{1} = \frac{100}{4} = 25\% \qquad\qquad \text{or} \qquad 0.25 \times 100 = 25\%$$

Percentages are quite easy to calculate, using multiplication.

$$4\% \text{ of } 900 \quad = \quad \frac{4}{100} \times 900 = 36 \qquad\qquad \text{or} \qquad 0.04 \times 900 = 36$$

The same method can be used to calculate:

- The amounts of VAT (20% of a total amount) to be added to an invoice, or the amount of a percentage discount (say 10% of a total amount) to be deducted from a total cost.

- The size of segments of pie charts, and other relative proportions (eg the percentage of total training costs incurred by a particular training programme).

- Changes (eg in sales, costs or output) from one period to another. If your accounts department processed 288 invoices in March and 300 invoices in April:

Its output grew by $\dfrac{300-288}{288}$ $=$ $\dfrac{12}{288} \times 100 = 4.2\%$

Task 5

A particular training programme costs £2,300. Your department's total training budget is £11,500.

(a) What percentage of the total budget is represented by this training programme?

(b) If you were to draw a pie chart showing this percentage, how many degrees (of a 360-degree circle) would it represent?

(c) If your department was eligible for a 15% discount on all training programmes over a value of £2,000, what would be the amount of the discount, and what would be the net amount payable?

Rounding

Rounding is a way of making numerical data easier to use by reducing the accuracy (or detail) of numbers to an appropriate level. If you are compiling average numbers of trainees on courses, for example, it may not be helpful to talk about 6.8 trainees being away from work at a given time: it would make more sense to round up to 7 (whole) trainees!

Similarly, if you have 7 trainees on courses costing a total of £699, and were asked for the 'cost per trainee', you know that you need to *divide* the cost by the number of trainees – and your calculator will tell you that you get £99.8571428. This is not particularly digestible or helpful information – particularly since in monetary units, you really only need two decimal places to give you pounds and pence.

To round to two decimal places, just look at the three numbers after the decimal place: in our example, 857. We are looking to round to the nearest 10, and this means rounding *up* to 860 (since 57 is closer to 60 than to 50). We can then knock off the final zero, to give us £99.86.

To round to three decimal places, look at the four numbers after the decimal place: 8571. We can round *down* to the nearest 10 (because 71 is closer to 70 than to 80): this gives us 8570 – and we can knock off the zero for the rounded number £99.857.

HOW IT WORKS

Back at Southfield Electronics, you have been asked to do some VAT calculations. You know that these calculations require the use of percentages, fractions, multiplication, division, addition, subtraction and rounding – so you are determined to work through the calculations carefully.

The *net amount* (sales price) shown on one invoice is £235.46. How much VAT should be charged on this amount? You know that VAT is 20% of the sales price and is rounded down to the nearest whole pence.

$$20\% \times £235.46 = \frac{20}{100} \times £235.46 = £47.092 \text{ (rounded to £47.09)}$$

The total amount (including VAT) will therefore be:

£235.46 + £47.09 = £282.55

On another invoice, you see that the *gross amount* (the total price of goods *plus* VAT) is £375.80. How much VAT is included in this price, and what is the net price of the goods? The total price includes the added 20%, so it totals 120% of the net price. The VAT is, of course, 20% of the total price. So:

$$\text{VAT} = \frac{20}{120} \times £375.80 = £62.6333 \text{ (rounded to £62.63)}$$

To get the net price of the goods, you then *subtract* the VAT from the VAT-inclusive price. £375.80 – £62.63 = £313.17.

Task 6

Goods with a list price of £2,450.00 are to be sent to a customer. The customer is allowed a trade discount of 15% and VAT is to be charged at 20%. What is the invoice total?

Averages

An AVERAGE is another way of reducing the level of detail in numerical data to a usable level, based on finding a value that is 'typical' or representative of a larger set of data.

There are three different types of averages.

- The *arithmetic mean* is found by adding up all the items in the set, then dividing the total by the number of items in the set.

  Say there were the following customer complaints about invoices over a six-month period.

January	February	March	April	May	June
0	26	0	5	3	2

  The average number of complaints is:

$$\frac{0 + 26 + 0 + 5 + 3 + 2}{6} = \frac{36}{6} = 6 \text{ per month}$$

  The problem with this is that *extremes* (like 26) distort the average: the actual monthly complaints are not as bad as 6 in five of the months – the average also disguises the fact that there was a real problem in February!

- The *median* is the middle value, when you arrange the data in ascending order. (If there is an even number of items, the median is mid-way between the middle two.) Here are our monthly complaints, re-ordered

| 0 | 0 | 2 | 3 | 5 | 26 |

↑
Median = 2.5

- The *mode* is the most frequently occurring value in a set of data. So the mode for our monthly complaints is 0.

Task 7

You are trying to compare the costs of training courses offered by two different providers, for a Continuing Professional Development plan.

The course costs are as follows.

	Provider 1	Provider 2
	£	£
Legal Compliance	250	340
Payroll Procedures	590	375
Spreadsheets	260	290
VAT Update	300	350
Effective Communication	200 per day*	210 per day**

  * 3 day course
** 2 ½ day course

Which provider offers the best value in terms of average cost? (Use both mean and median values, and comment on the differences.)

Selecting the right numeracy tool

One of the tricky things about being set numerical tasks is that they are often set in words! You have to work out what numerical operation is required to get the information you are being asked for.

- To calculate work output 'per' month, for example, you need to *divide* the total output by the number of months under consideration.

- On the other hand, if you are asked to calculate work output in a particular month, you may need to *add* up the output of different team members in that month.

- If you are told how many tasks a team member can complete in an hour, and the number of hours she worked in a day, you will need to *multiply* the hours by the hourly output to get her total daily output. You could *multiply* this by the number of days worked in the month, to get this team member's monthly output.

- If you know the total monthly output and the monthly output of each team member, you could also calculate the *percentage* of the total monthly output represented by each team member: team member output *divided by* total output *multiplied* by 100. For ease of use, you might *round* this percentage to one or two decimal places. (You could then re-calculate them as percentages of a 360º circle and draw a handy pie chart, to motivate the team with a bit of healthy competition!)

- Now, say that a team member's time costs '£50 per half day' when she is away on a training course, and that she does '1 day' of training per month'. How would you manipulate this information to calculate the total overtime cost over a *year*? First of all, notice the different units we've been given to work with: half days, days, months, years. Let's get them all into a common unit: days.

  £50 per half day = £100 *per day*.
  1 day per month × 12 months in a year = 12 *days* per year.
  Now it's easy: 12 *days* × £100 *per day* = £1,200 per year.

- What if you then found you were eligible for a 10% discount from the training provider because your spend exceeded a particular threshold? You would have to calculate the *percentage* (10/100 × total spend) – and then *deduct* it from the total.

Accuracy in numerical tasks

One of the great problems in accounting and payroll work is the need for a high level of accuracy – particularly avoiding silly mistakes such as adding a number instead of subtracting it, using the wrong tables or making an arithmetical error. This is also a problem in assessments! So what can you do to minimise the risk of errors?

- Always check your work before finishing and submitting it.

- Don't see tasks as mechanical processes: try to understand what the numbers represent, so that you know (a) what needs to be done with them and (b) whether answers are plausible or likely.

- Perform credibility checks, such as using mental arithmetic to see approximately what you expect the answer to be.

Task 8

Calculate the cost of each employee's travel expenses as a percentage of the total cost of travel expenses. Calculate the percentage to 3 decimal places.

	Travel expense
	£
Anne	45
Jaitinder	71
Benjamin	86
Chloe	32
Vimal	<u>59</u>
	293

CHAPTER OVERVIEW

- Communication is, at its most basic, the transmission or exchange of information. It is at the core of the role of the accounting and payroll functions within an organisation.

- You are required to demonstrate that you can communicate effectively, clearly and appropriately in a range of situations. This broadly means: using appropriate formats; observing format conventions and house style; presenting information neatly and professionally; ensuring that content is technically correct and clearly understandable (bearing in mind the needs and capacities of your audience); projecting an appropriate corporate image; and achieving your purpose in communicating.

- When planning a communication, you want to PASS: know your Purpose and Audience, and use the right Structure and Style

- Keep It Short and Simple (KISS) is an important guideline for business communication.

- The formality appropriate for business communication is considerably greater than you might use in non-work settings, and you must bear this in mind.

- You are required to demonstrate a range of numeracy skills appropriate to this level, including (but not limited to) addition and subtraction, multiplication and division, fractions, percentages, and rounding to a certain number of decimal places.

- Other important numeracy skills are (a) working out what numerical operation is required to get the information you are being asked for, (b) checking the accuracy of your calculations and (c) formatting your work in a clear way.

Keywords

Communication – a method of putting across a message and ensuring that the message is understood

Jargon – technical terminology which may not be understood by non-specialists

Corporate image – the image of itself which the organisation seeks to project to the outside world

Corporate identity – guidelines for how the organisation presents itself visually in its communications

Fraction – a ratio of two numbers – for example, $1/4$ means 'one part in four'.

Percentage – a proportion or rate per hundred parts – for example, $20\% = 20$ parts per hundred or $1/5$

Average – a value that is typical, representative or 'middling' for a set of data

TEST YOUR LEARNING

Test 1

Suggest five different purposes you might have in communicating in a business context.

Test 2

What would be the most appropriate method of communication in each of the following circumstances?

(a) Explaining to a customer that a cash discount that has been deducted was not valid, as the invoice was not paid within the discount period

(b) Requesting customer balances from a colleague in the sales ledger department

(c) Arranging your holiday period with the HR manager

(d) A complaint to a supplier regarding the delivery times of goods, which are not as agreed

(e) Information to be provided to the sales director regarding the breakdown of sales geographically for the last two years.

Test 3

What do you understand by the term 'feedback' in communication, and why is it important?

Test 4

A newly-recruited colleague brings you her job description, which states that she needs to be able to 'communicate effectively, clearly and appropriately' in her role. Communication was not included in her induction training, and she is about to have a meeting with her supervisor to identify her learning needs for the next three months. She asks you to explain what 'communicating effectively, clearly and appropriately' means. What will you tell her?

Test 5

As a payroll assistant:

(a) You have calculated one employee's weekly wages as a counter assistant in a fast food shop as £1,089.67.

(b) You have calculated another employee's gross pay for the year to date as £6,211.67. It is Month 3 (ie the employee has received three months' salary), and you know that his annual salary is in the region of £25,000 per year.

(c) You have calculated another employee's gross pay for the month as £1,545. Her annual salary is £18,000, but she has done 30 hours of overtime (at £15 per hour), in connection with the preparation for the annual audit.

Do these results look right to you? If not, what might alert you to the possibility of a miscalculation?

Test 6

What do you understand by the mnemonics 'PASS' and 'KISS'?

Test 7

What is 'corporate identity' and how might it impact on your business communications?

Test 8

A junior colleague shows you a draft of an email to the Purchasing Director of a company which has recently expressed an interest in your products. He asks you to edit any words or phrases you think are inappropriate. The draft appears as follows.

EMAIL

To: hgwells@retail.com
From: acdoyle@southfield.co.uk
Date: *[Today's date]*
Subject: Your recent enquiry
Attach: Sales brochure.pdf

Hi, Hugh.
Thanks for your msg re our products. Its cool that you were able to come and see our display at the Home Entertainment Trade Fair. More than happy to help with further info.

IMHO, our company's one of the best in the field, and our product's have recently one an award as Retail Product of the Year.

I've attached a brochure what details our full product range, it includes prices and terms of trade. Having received it, I will contact you soon to see if you'd like to place an order.

In the meantime, me and the sales team are availble to answer any questions you may have, it'd be gr8 to hear from you.

Cheers.

Arthur

Redraft the email, making any corrections you see fit, and make a note of how you would explain your changes to Arthur, to help him improve his communication skills.

Test 9

It is 15 May and you have just received an invoice for 2,000 kg of raw materials. Inclusive of sales tax (VAT) the invoice totals £4,580 and the sales tax rate is 20%.

Next month you need another 2,000 kg of the same raw material but you know the sales tax exclusive material price is set to rise by 3% by the start of June.

What will the sales tax value be on the 2,000 kg to be purchased in June?

Test 10

Your Accounts department processed £16,600 worth of invoices in January and £20,916 worth of invoices in February. What percentage increase in revenue does this represent?

chapter 5:
PRESENTING INFORMATION

chapter coverage 📖

In this chapter, you will develop the knowledge and skills required to produce professional informal business reports, letters, emails and memos. You will learn to use standard formats correctly and effectively, within organisational guidelines.

The chapter explains how you should use the documents provided in the assessment to determine the style and layout of your answers to the tasks. It also explains how to structure informal reports, letters and other business documents and the appropriate use of diagrams and charts.

You should use the tasks within the chapter and the questions at the end to practise and develop your skills.

The topics covered are:

- ✐ Choosing communication formats
- ✐ House style, guidelines and policies
- ✐ Informal business reports
- ✐ Using diagrams and charts
- ✐ Business letters
- ✐ Memos and business emails

CHOOSING COMMUNICATION FORMATS

There are a variety of possible methods of communication for presenting business information, and you must select the most appropriate method for the circumstances, for the target audience, and for the type of message that is to be relayed.

Face-to-face communication (in meetings, interviews, discussions or presentations) allows you to express yourself fully, to be sensitive to the other person, to take advantage of on-the-spot question-and-answer, and to gain immediate feedback to make sure your message is getting across. However, a face-to-face meeting is often not possible due to time constraints or physical location. It is also often the case that, particularly with a complex subject, it is better to communicate the details in writing so that the recipient has time to consider the details and complexities and has a copy for reference/confirmation.

If immediate feedback or personal sensitivity is required but face-to-face communication is not feasible, the next best option is a *telephone call*.

Short notes are good methods of passing on information and providing a reminder (eg asking someone to carry out a task) in informal settings (eg among colleagues).

Letters are often used in formal, person-to-person business communication where urgency (given the lead time for postal delivery) is not a factor. Letters can be made confidential by stating 'private and confidential' on the envelope and at the top of the letter, so that only the target recipient should open the message.

Informal reports are often used in business communication to convey larger amounts of information in a clear, structured, easy-to-use way.

Memos are a standardised, efficient way of sending messages within an organisation. They may be the approved internal format for notes and short informal reports.

EMAIL is extremely versatile: it can be used to send notes, memos, letters, reports, forms and all sorts of other messages. Email has the huge advantages of speed (provided the recipient picks up the message when it is sent) and electronic format (so it can be easily filed, edited, copied and sent to multiple recipients all at once). It can also have other documents (reports, diagrams, schedules and so on) 'attached', if this would be helpful in backing up the main message.

HOUSE STYLE, GUIDELINES AND POLICIES

As we saw in Chapter 4, business communication needs to be more planned, more formal and more efficient than everyday communication, in order to:

- Make best use of the time of all parties involved

- Avoid misunderstandings or communication failures, which could be detrimental to the achievement of deadlines and objectives

- Establish and maintain positive relationships with colleagues, customers, suppliers and other stakeholders in the business.

For this reason, organisations often issue guidelines for their staff on how to use various communication methods efficiently and effectively, and how external messages should be presented.

Communication policies

Organisations often publish policies and guidelines on how to use – and how not to *abuse* – communication tools such as the telephone and emails.

There may be restrictions on making personal calls or using email and internet for personal purposes at work. There will often be strict warnings about the unacceptability of offensive or illegal content in messages – although we hope this would be common sense! In an accounting and finance setting, there will almost certainly be policies about confidentiality: what information can and cannot be given, to whom, and by what means, to protect the integrity and security of information.

There may also be helpful guidelines for staff about issues such as: data security when using email (eg the use of anti-virus software); the rules of email 'etiquette'; when to use (and not to use) email; what 'signature' information should be added to the end of emails; and so on.

If any such policies or guidelines are provided in your assessment case study, remember that they are there for a reason – and adhere to them when tackling communication tasks!

Task 1

What are some of the key reasons for having policy guidelines for when and how employees should use email in their communications at work?

House style

Organisations seek to communicate a consistent, coherent image to the outside world – and, ideally, also one that reflects the corporate identity, self-image and style. If every member of the organisation presents letters and emails differently, according to their own preferences, a consistent image will be difficult to maintain!

'HOUSE STYLE' is an expression of how the organisation wants to present itself in its communications. It may include aspects such as the use of standardised letterheads and memo pads; how letters and memos are laid out; what headings and formats are used for reports; and the logos, typefaces and colours used as part of the corporate identity. It may also include more subtle aspects such as a tendency towards informality or formality in the tone of writing, or creativity or traditionalism in the style of presentation.

House style may be developed informally, as 'the way we do things around here', which people pick up through modelling their messages on existing examples. In your assessment, for example, you may have to model your letterhead, layout and presentation on specimen documents provided in the case study material.

House style may also be formally expressed in guidelines and rules for communication – and if this is the case, in your work organisation *or* in the assessment case study, you should seek to adhere to the guidelines set for you.

HOW IT WORKS

At Southfield Electronics, there is a House Style manual for all communications sent to external parties.

Standardised stationery is available for handwritten and word-processed documents – and also for email messages. The corporate letterhead appears as follows.

SOUTHFIELD ELECTRONICS LTD

Tomorrow's technology for today's homes

Micro House
Newtown Technology Park
Innovation Way
Middx NT3 OPN

Every email must be 'signed off' with a standard block of text called a 'signature block', which is inserted automatically by the email software:

[Sender's Name]
[Sender's Position]

Southfield Electronics Ltd
Micro House, Newtown Technology park
Innovation Way, Middx NT3 OPN, UK

Tel: +44 (0)20x xxx xxxx * Fax: +44 (0)20x xxx xxxx * Web:
www.southfield.com

This message and any attachments are confidential and may contain information that is subject to copyright. If you are not the intended recipient, please notify us immediately by replying to this message and then delete it from your system. While we take reasonable precautions to prevent computer viruses, we cannot accept responsibility for viruses transmitted to your computer and it is your responsibility to make all necessary checks. We may monitor email traffic data and the content of emails to ensure efficient operation of our business, for security, for staff training and for other administrative purposes.

General guidelines for effective written communication

We have already looked at these in Chapter 4: be ready to apply them to specific formats such as reports, letters, memos and emails. In order to create clearer communications *and* foster more effective working relationships:

- Take into account your *purpose* in writing: what are your aims and objectives? What response or action do you want as a result of your message?

- Take into account the *requirements of your target recipient* or audience: their information needs and capacities (including their limited time, and familiarity/unfamiliarity with technical jargon).

- *Structure* your communication in such a way as to make it easy to read and understand

- *Keep it short and simple* (KISS) and aim for clarity and ease of understanding

- *Present* your material in a way that demonstrates professionalism and reflects the desired image of the organisation.

We will now look at some of the main tools for presenting information in the accounting and finance environment.

INFORMAL BUSINESS REPORTS

'Report' is a general term, which covers a wide range of formats. If you inform someone verbally or in writing of facts, events, actions you have taken, or suggestions you wish to make – you are reporting. In this sense, you can make a report in a meeting or phone call, letter, memo or email.

If you are asked for an INFORMAL REPORT, however, this will usually mean a relatively short written document, in which information is presented in a direct and structured way.

Informal report structure

A formal report can be a massive, complex and highly-structured affair, presenting and analysing high-level concepts and information. An informal report is generally used for less complex reporting tasks, so it does not require elaborate referencing, structuring and layout. However, it still needs to have a clear structure and layout, to help the user to 'navigate' through the information.

Standard elements of report structure are shown a little later.

Informal report style

There are some important points to note about the written style of an informal business report.

The language is still more *formal* than that used in everyday speech, or in informal messages to colleagues. Avoid slang and colloquialisms. Write grammatically in full sentences. Do not take short cuts: use 'there is' rather than 'there's', and 'I have' rather than 'I've'.

The key objective is *ease of understanding*, and ease of *navigation through the information*, for the user.

- Avoid technical language for non-technical users.

- Organise your material logically – especially if it is designed to be persuasive, leading up to a conclusion or recommendation!

- Signal relevant topics by using appropriate headings.

- Consider using tables or diagrams, where this would be *helpful* in highlighting important points (such as comparisons or trends), or in organising raw data (eg into a table).

- Consider removing background or supporting detail into an *APPENDIX or appendices*: attaching relevant documents at the end of the report, in order to keep its main body concise and flowing.

REPORT TITLE ('Report on [topic]')

To: Requester/recipient of the report

From: Compiler/writer of the report

Date: Date of submission

(Alternatively, these details may be written in a brief Introduction section. Follow any template or guidance you are given.)

The body of the report, structured in sections, with clear headings.

Section heading: as dictated by the report brief

Report sections may reflect a list of topics you were asked to cover in the report 'brief', or request for information. If you are given a number of issues to report on, it makes sense to use these as your report sections.

Section heading: as dictated by the task

If you are asked to investigate an issue, give your findings and make recommendations, it would make sense to have sections headed: Background; Investigation; Findings; and Recommendations (or similar).

Section heading: as dictated by the subject matter

A subject will often have topic areas to provide report headings. You might report on a process, for example, under the headings of its various stages or steps. You might report on data security under the headings of particular security risks (viruses, phishing, systems failure, loss of data).

Conclusions and recommendations

Check that you have included any specific requirements, such as *recommendations* for action. If there are no such requirements, consider whether it would be helpful to the report user to have a *summary* (a roundup of the report's main thrust) or a *conclusion* (what facts, decisions or options the report has led to).

Appendices

Supporting data and documents can be attached to the report, where useful. Such documents should be numbered and referred to in the body of the report, so the user can locate the data: eg '… based on September sales forecasts (See Appendix 1)' or '… as set out in the attached Schedule (Appendix 2)'.

HOW IT WORKS

You have been at Southfield Electronics for a while now, and you are becoming frustrated by the tendency for staff members to 'cut corners' on organisational policies and procedures, such as correct authorisation of cheque requisitions; respect for the confidentiality of other staff members' personal details; and attendance at fire evacuation drills.

You mention this in conversation with Jenny Faulkner, the financial accountant, and she asks you to write an informal report covering: incidences of non-compliance, reasons for concern, and how Southfield can improve compliance. You draft the following.

SOUTHFIELD ELECTRONICS LTD

REPORT: COMPLIANCE WITH POLICY & PROCEDURE

1   Introduction

This report was compiled by Your Name, Accounts Clerk, at the request of Jenny Faulkner, Financial Accountant, and submitted on 3rd September 20X0.

2   Non-compliance with policy and procedure

In recent months, I have witnessed several cases in which staff members have failed to comply with formal policies and procedures.

- Cheque requisition forms have had to be returned to the originators because they were incorrectly completed or authorised. (See copies attached: Appendix 1)
- There is an apparent lack of respect for the confidentiality of other staff members' personal details, in verbal and written communication with third parties.
- Staff members fail to take part in fire evacuation drills, and when they do take part, fail to comply with proper procedures (eg by taking lifts and leaving fire doors open). (See the Safety Officer's report on the most recent drill: Appendix 2.)

3   Reasons for concern

I believe these 'lapses' in compliance are of concern, for several reasons.

Policies and procedures, such as the ones mentioned, have been put in place to ensure the efficiency of operations such as cheque requisition; the confidentiality of information which may be used to the detriment of the organisation and/or its staff; and the safety of staff and visitors in the event of an emergency.

Non-compliance in such areas jeopardises efficiency (by necessitating re-work), data security and personal safety.

By themselves these may be small things, but I believe they may reflect a culture of 'corner cutting' which may eventually result in more serious consequences.

4   How Southfield can improve compliance

I would like to make the following recommendations for management's consideration.

- All staff should be reminded of their responsibility to comply with organisational policies and procedures.
- Where necessary, training should be given to reinforce awareness and competence in relevant procedures.

> - Managers at all levels should seek to monitor and enforce compliance more strictly, and to model compliance in their own conduct.
>
> I hope this information is helpful, and I would be willing to discuss it further – and to present more detailed evidence of my observations – at your convenience.
>
> **Appendix 1:** Incorrectly completed cheque requisition forms (attached)
> **Appendix 2:** Safety Officer's Report for August 20X0 (attached)

USING DIAGRAMS AND CHARTS

If you are preparing a report (or perhaps preparing slides for a presentation), you may need to use visual aids of some kind. Diagrams are useful in conveying large amounts of data more accessibly and in adding interest and appeal to a document.

In addition to the numerical competences required to organise your data, there are some key principles of effective 'graphic' communication.

- Give each diagram or chart a concise and meaningful title.

- Cite the source of the data, where relevant.

- Clearly label all elements of the diagram, either on the diagram itself, or in a separate 'key' to the colours or symbols used.

- Keep textual elements (labels, explanatory notes) brief.

- Keep the presentation as simple as possible: cut down on unnecessary lines and elements, to avoid overcrowding, clutter and confusion.

- Make the diagram large enough so that it is easy to read.

Let's look briefly at some examples of visual elements you might use in an informal report.

Tables

Tables are a good way of *organising information*. The use of columns and rows allows the data to be classified under appropriate headings, clearly organised and labelled, totalled up in various ways (across rows or down columns) and so on.

You might use a table format to organise data about a list of trainees, say, as follows.

Staff member	Training undertaken	Training provider	Duration of training (days)	Cost of training
John				
Amy				
Fred				
		Total:		

Bar charts

Bar charts are useful for *showing or comparing magnitudes* or sizes of items: for example, sales revenue or expenditure on a month-by-month basis, or training costs per department.

- The diagram needs to be labelled to indicate what it shows.

- The positions of the bars are labelled to show what they represent (eg months or departments).

- The height of the bars, drawn against a specified scale, indicate the magnitudes of the different items (monetary value or number).

- The bars can be subdivided to show components of the total magnitudes (eg breakdown of monthly expenditure by department or category).

Sales Revenue 20X0

Pie charts

Pie charts are useful for showing the relative sizes of *component elements* of a *total value or amount*, represented by the 360° of the circle or 'pie'. An example might be showing the breakdown of the time you spend on different tasks during a day, or the breakdown of monthly sales revenue by product or customer.

Step 1: Calculate each item as a fraction and/or percentage of the whole. (If handling emails takes you five hours out of your 40-hour week, say, that's 5/40 or 1/8 or 12.5%.)

Step 2: Translate each fraction/percentage into fractions of a circle. (The 'slice' occupied by handling emails would be 1/8 of the pie.) If you want to draw very accurately, using geometric instruments, you would calculate the exact number of degrees of the circle occupied by each slice, as a fraction or percentage of 360°. (1/8 × 360° = 45°)

Step 3:   Draw a circle, and divide it up using the fractions (or, to be more accurate, degrees) calculated for each slice.

Step 4:   Label each slice with what it represents, and its percentage of the total. Check that it adds up to 100%!

HOW IT WORKS

Jenny Faulkner has asked you to report on the breakdown of your 40-hour working week, to check whether your being a 'shared resource' for the assistant financial accountants and payroll manager is working.

You work out that in an average week, emails take 5 hours (12.5%); your work on payroll takes 20 hours (50%); and your work on ledgers takes 15 hours (37.5%). In presenting this data in your report to Jenny, you decide it will be most helpful in graphic form. You calculate as follows:

5/40 × 360   =   45º   (1/8 of the pie)
20/40× 360   =   180º   (1/2 of the pie)
15/40 × 360   =   135º   (3/8 of the pie)

And you draw the following simple pie chart, for inclusion in your report.

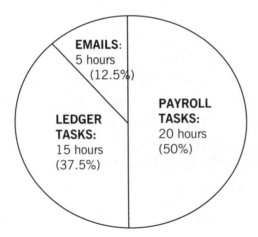

Line graphs

Line graphs are useful for showing the relationship between two variables (represented by the horizontal and vertical axes of the graph), by plotting points and joining them up with straight or curved lines. These are particularly useful for demonstrating trends, such as the increase in departmental output as more time/money is invested in training and development – or fluctuations in revenue or expenditure (or other values) over time.

Here's a very simple example.

Average waiting time for processing of petty cash claims on different days of the week

Such a graph could be used to highlight variations in work throughput.

Task 2

The table below shows a company's sales figures for the first six months of 20X0.

Product	Jan £000	Feb £000	Mar £000	Apr £000	May £000	Jun £000	Total £000
A	800	725	725	400	415	405	
B	210	210	180	150	175	160	
C	25	50	60	95	125	140	
Total							

(a)   Add up the rows and columns to insert the totals.

(b)   What kind of graph or chart would you use to show the fluctuations of monthly sales figures across the six months? Draw it.

(c)   What kind of graph or chart would you use to show the proportion of total sales represented by each product? Draw it.

BUSINESS LETTERS

A letter is a very flexible and versatile medium of written, person-to-person communication. It can be used for many business purposes: requesting, supplying and confirming information and instructions; offering and accepting goods and services; conveying and acknowledging satisfaction and dissatisfaction (eg complaint and adjustment letters); and explaining what else is in an information package via a covering letter.

The modern business letter contains various *standard elements* and you will need to know what these are and where they are located on the page. Below, you will see a skeleton format and a full example.

Letterheads (the logo, name and contact details of the organisation sending the letter) are often pre-printed on office stationery, or built into word processor templates. If not (eg in your assessment project), remember to reproduce the name and address details given at the top of the letter page.

Check that for any letter you write, you have included:

- The name and address of the target recipient

- Date

- Greeting (or 'salutation')

- Subject heading (a brief, helpful 'cue' to what the letter is about)

- The main body of the letter

- Sign-off (or 'complimentary close')

- Signature. If an assistant is signing a letter on behalf of the writer, the writer's name must be preceded by 'For' (or its equivalent from legal terminology: 'pp' which stands for per procurationem)

- Enclosure reference: 'enc' (or 'encs' for more than one item), if something other than the letter is included in the same envelope – such as a cheque, price list or leaflet

- Copy reference: 'copies to' or 'cc' plus the names of any third parties to whom copies of the letter have been sent.

ORGANISATION LETTERHEAD
(may be pre-printed on stationery)

Confidentiality warning *(if applicable)*

Recipient's name
Designation
Address   Date

Greeting (salutation),

Subject heading

Introductory paragraph: explaining the context and reason for writing.

The main body of the letter, set out with clear separate paragraphs for each sub-topic or new phase of your message.

The content may be tackled in chronological order (if you are narrating or explaining a sequence of events, say) or in any other appropriate order for the subject matter.

Closing paragraph: summarising the content and purpose of the message, and making clear what course of action (if any) you want the reader to take. Putting this last makes it most impactful and memorable.

Complimentary close *(matched to the salutation),*

Author's signature (handwritten)

Author's name
Author's position

Enclosure reference *(if something is in the envelope with the letter)*
Copy reference *(if a copy of the letter has been sent to another person)*

SOUTHFIELD ELECTRONICS LTD

Tomorrow's technology for today's homes

Micro House
Newtown Technology Park
Innovation Way
Middx NT3 OPN

Confidential

J M Bloggs
Administrator
Wallend Retail Ltd
Wood Lane Industrial Estate
Sussex BN1 4PW

3 September 20X0

Dear Mr Bloggs,

Account No 0139742

Thank you for your letter of 28 August 20X0 regarding credit payments owing to your account as a result of product returns.

I have looked into the matter that you raised and I am afraid that your earlier letter of 26 July was indeed overlooked, due to the temporary absence of the member of staff to whom you addressed it.

I apologise for the delay in processing your credit payment. I have arranged for your account to be credited with the sum of £346.99, and I enclose a print-out of your account status confirming the balance.

If you have any further queries, please do not hesitate to contact me.

Yours sincerely,

Your Name

pp Kellie McDonald
Assistant Financial Accountant

enc.
cc: Kellie McDonald

Appropriate salutations

You need to demonstrate that you can use an appropriate greeting or salutation for the type of relationship you have with the person you are writing to: this may be formal or informal, in recognition of the other person's status, the familiarity of the relationship, and the customs of the organisation (such as calling managers by their first names – or not!).

By convention, the following greetings (or 'salutations') and sign-offs (or 'complimentary closes') should be used together, and you need to demonstrate that you can match them correctly.

Salutation	Close	Context
Dear Sir/Madam/Sirs (name not used)	Yours faithfully	Formal situations Recipients not known
Dear Dr/Mr/Mrs/Ms Bloggs (formal name used)	Yours sincerely	Established relationships Friendly but respectful (eg with superiors, customers, suppliers)
Dear Joe/Josephine	Yours sincerely Kind regards	More personal, informal relationships (eg with colleagues)

Task 3

You have been asked to write a letter to the following people. What salutations and closes will you use?

(a) The accounts department of a firm you are dealing with for the first time.

(b) A female customer whose name you know to be Georgia Brown, but whose marital status you do not know.

(c) A sales representative called Mark Stein, whom you know well and with whom you are on first name terms.

(d) The managing director of your firm, whose name is Sir Joshua Holmes.

Professional image

A letter may be the first contact a person has with your organisation, so it needs to make a positive impression. As discussed in Chapter 3, this generally means: legibility, neatness, conciseness and businesslike tone. If a letter is handwritten, you will need to minimise crossings out (or Tippex). If it is word processed, it will still require attention to spelling errors, 'typos' and other problems (such as faint or blotchy printing) which may spoil the image of professionalism you are trying to create.

House style

An organisation may have its own stationery and letterhead. In your assessment, remember to duplicate any letterhead shown in specimen letters from the case study organisation – or devise your own professional-looking letterhead from the name and contact details given.

House style or custom may also dictate where the standard letter elements are arranged on the page.

- Our example shows what is called a 'semi-blocked' layout, with the date at the top right-hand side of the page, and the subject header centred.

- You will often see the simpler 'fully blocked' style, with everything against the left-hand margin.

At work, you should follow the layout used in your own organisation. In your assessment, you should follow the style used in the case study organisation: look for where the standard elements are placed in any specimen letters provided.

Well structured

A letter (and indeed, any written message) should have a beginning, a middle and an end.

- The opening paragraph is important, because the reader will not be as familiar with the context or reason for the letter as you are! Offer a brief explanation of why you are writing, an acknowledgement of relevant correspondence received, or other introductory background details.

- The middle paragraph(s) should contain the substance of your message. If you are making several points, start a new paragraph with each, so that the reader can digest each part of your message in turn.

- The closing paragraph is important, because it is the best opportunity to make clear to the reader what you hope to have achieved. Summarise your point briefly, or make clear exactly what response is required.

Task 4

Suggest some opening lines for the following letter situations.

(a)   You are replying to an agreement you made by phone to send someone a brochure detailing your services.

(b)   You have had a phone message from one of your sales reps, George Brown, saying that a person wants to enquire about job openings in the accounts department, and would like to be contacted by mail.

Suggest some closing lines for the following letter situations.

(c)   You already have a meeting scheduled to discuss the matter further.

(d)   You have just provided the person with answers to questions.

Clearly written

Again, remember the KISS principles we discussed in Chapter 4. Your written style needs to be helpfully structured (in well-spaced paragraphs), easy to read, unambiguous, free of jargon, free of cliché (without meaningless 'stock' phrases), and concise (without unnecessary words).

We can't really teach you to do this. You will have to develop your skills at letter writing by modelling your style on the examples given in this Workbook and in the assessment case study – and by evaluating what does and does not work in the letters you encounter.

MEMOS AND BUSINESS EMAILS

Memos

A MEMO or 'memorandum' performs the same function internally as a letter does in external communication by an organisation. It can be used for reports, brief messages or 'notes' and any kind of internal communication that is most easily or clearly conveyed in writing.

Memos are generally written on stationery pre-printed with appropriate headings – or typed into a word-processor template. The standardised headings are designed to make writing more efficient, given that the message is for internal use.

The following shows the standard elements of memo format.

MEMO

To: [Recipient's name, designation]   **Reference:** [File reference]

From: [Sender's name, designation]   **Date:** [In full]

Subject: [Concise statement of main theme or topic of message]

The main text of the memo is set out in correct, concise, readily understandable English, in spaced paragraphs following a clear, logical structure. Note that no inside address, salutation or complimentary close are required.

Signature or initials [optional]

cc: [To indicate recipient(s) of copies of the memo, if any]
enc: [To indicate accompanying material, if any]

Nowadays, memos have generally been replaced by internal email messages, which have much the same features – except that you are typing into an electronic form created by email software.

HOW IT WORKS

Following your informal report on non-compliance with Southfield Electronics' policies and procedures, Jenny Faulkner has been investigating, and one morning you receive the following memo.

 SOUTHFIELD ELECTRONICS LTD

MEMO

To: Your Name, Accounts Clerk
From: Jenny Faulkner, Financial Accountant
Date: 11 September 20X0
Subject   Abuse of telephone procedures

I have been looking into instances of non-compliance with procedures, and I believe I have identified an additional matter that would be worth investigating further. As you know, our telephone costs have risen significantly over the last quarter, and I have identified three main causes.

1.   There are more telephones in the office than are necessary for efficient communication.

2.   Staff have become accustomed to making personal calls on office apparatus.

3.   Many calls are made at expensive charge rates and at unnecessary length.

I would like the accounts team to come up with some ideas for action to prevent further cost increases. Is this something that you might be interested in taking on as a project?

Meanwhile, let me know if you have any initial thoughts on the matter.

Thanks.

JF

Task 5

(a)   Write Jenny a brief memo replying to the memo sent to you in the 'How It Works' section above.

(b)   Write a brief letter to an office equipment company (TeleComs Ltd, 6 Park Way, Brighton, Sussex BN3 4PW) asking for information about models and costs of electronic switchboards and devices for the logging of telephone calls from handsets.

Email

EMAIL is a method for sending electronic messages from one computer to another, either internally within the workplace or to an external party. Email is easy to use, extremely fast and relatively cheap. It is also particularly flexible, because photos, diagrams, computer files or spreadsheets can be sent (with the email as a kind of 'covering letter') as attachments.

To use email, you simply log onto the email software (the most common being Microsoft Outlook), and press 'Create email' or 'New mail'. This presents you with a standard email 'page', which looks a bit like a memo form with extra option buttons!

If you have access to email facilities, you simply type data into the fields on the on-screen email page. When the recipient receives your message (and/or when you print it out), the various headers will be included in the print-out, and the sender address and date will be inserted automatically.

If you are asked to draft the text of an email as an assessment task, however, you may need to include the header elements, to demonstrate that you know what an email looks like. A standard format may be given to you in the case study, in which case – use it! Otherwise, the standard elements for an email are much like a memo.

EMAIL

To: [Recipient's email address: name@company.co.uk or similar]

Cc: [Email addresses of parties to whom the message is copied]

From: [Sender's email address]

Date: [Today's date]

Subject: Concise statement of main theme or topic of message.

Attach: [Name of file attached to the message]

The main text of the email should be written in correct, concise, readily understandable English, in spaced paragraphs following a clear, logical structure and a simple format – avoid the use of **bold**, underlined, *italic* or CAPITALISED text (capitals in an email give an impression of you shouting, which is not professional).

Name/initials (optional)

Signature block (inserted automatically, if used)

Using email effectively

Email is so widespread, it is easy to forget that it has some limitations as a medium of communication!

It is not as secure as you might think (particularly if you accidentally send it to the wrong address or multiple addresses): think carefully before using it for private and confidential messages.

Email is fast and easy to use: think carefully before 'dashing off' messages which may damage relationships (eg by being offensive or inappropriately informal) or have practical implications (eg making commitments to a customer or supplier which you can't later fulfil).

As some email programmes remove formatting, it is best to avoid anything fancy in an email that you send, such as **bold**, underlined, *italic* or CAPITALISED text, since these may not actually be seen by the recipient. Capitals in particular give the wrong impression, usually that the sender is annoyed and is shouting at the recipient. Also to be avoided because of the unprofessional impression they give are 'emoticons' such as smileys ☹.

When you have finished the message, always check it through thoroughly: once it has been sent there is no retrieving it!

You should familiarise yourself with the email format (and any guidelines for use) of your organisation – and look out for specimen emails, email templates and email policy guidelines in the assessment case study.

Making best use of the subject line

The subject line is more or less compulsory in emails (sometimes the software won't let you send a message without one), because if you don't signal what the message is about, the recipient may think it is SPAM (an unsolicited mass marketing message) or some kind of fake message carrying a computer virus: any message without a relevant subject line *should* be deleted unread!

The subject line is helpful in letting the recipient know whether the message is worth reading; whether it is high or low priority; and whether it has been directed to the right person (or needs to be forwarded). It also directs the recipient to the subject of the message, like a very brief 'executive summary', so that (s)he can be mentally prepared, and read the message more efficiently.

So use the subject line wisely. Use a short phrase that will most effectively convey the seriousness, relevance and topic of the message to a user who may not be expecting it. ('Hi there' or 'read this' probably won't do the job...)

If you are replying directly to an email sent to you (by pressing the 'reply' button), the email software will insert the subject line: 'RE: [the subject of the original message]'. So if you reply to a message 'Monthly totals', the subject line will automatically read: 'RE: Monthly totals'. You might bear this in mind, for authenticity, if you are replying to another email in your assessment.

HOW IT WORKS

Back at Southfield Electronics, you are working on your analysis of the customers that have been allocated to you. Just to check that you are doing it correctly, you would like a copy of an analysis which your colleague Amy Laval has already completed. You send her a quick email.

EMAIL	
Date:	[inserted automatically]
To:	alaval@southfield.co.uk
From:	yname@southfield.co.uk
Subject:	Customer analysis

Amy,

I'd be grateful if you could send me a copy of a customer analysis that you have already completed, so that I can check that I am doing it correctly.

Thanks.

Your Name

Task 6

Compose an email from Amy to you, in reply to your email to her in the 'How It Works' example above.

CHAPTER OVERVIEW

- Workplace communication methods include face-to-face discussion, telephone calls, informal notes, memos, emails, letters and informal reports.

- Organisations often issue guidelines for staff on how to use various communication methods efficiently and effectively, and how external messages should be presented. 'House style' is an expression of how the organisation wants to present itself in its communications, and house style conventions and guidelines should be adhered to, to ensure consistency and coherence.

- Informal reports are relatively short written documents, in which information is presented in a direct and structured way. They should follow a clear logical structure, and be written in an easy-to-understand and appropriately businesslike (relatively formal) style.

- Diagrams and charts (including bar charts, line graphs, pie charts and flow charts) may be used in reports to illustrate key points of data. They should be carefully drawn and labelled for ease of use.

- Business letters are highly versatile for person-to-person written communication. They contain various standard elements. You will need to know what these are and where they are located on the page in different 'house style' layouts. It is particularly important to use appropriate salutations (greetings) and closes.

- Memos cover a wide range of internal written messages. They are generally written on stationery with pre-prepared standard headings.

- Email is a method for sending written message from one computer to another. Email software, like memo stationery, has pre-prepared headings into which you can input sender/recipient and subject information. You need to make good use of the subject line.

- Regardless of format, all reports, letters, memos and emails must conform to house style guidelines and the attributes of effective communication.

Keywords

Email – an electronic method of sending a note, letter, memo or other information via computer

House style – the distinctive way an organisation seeks to present itself in its communications

Informal report – a relatively short written document, in which information is presented in a direct and structured way

Appendix – a separate section attached to a report, with supporting data or documents referred to in the report

Memo – a structured message sent within an organisation via internal mail

TEST YOUR LEARNING

Test 1

For each of the following situations, which would be the most appropriate method of communication?

(a)   Detailing a telephone message left by a supplier for a colleague

(b)   Informing an employee that his work has not been up to standard recently

(c)   Requesting a customer's sales ledger account balance from the credit controller

(d)   Requesting production details for the last month from the factory manager where the factory is situated five miles away

(e)   Sending monthly variances to the sales manager

Test 2

Identify four elements of 'house style' that you would look out for in the format of an organisation's communications, if you wanted to prepare your own communications in that style.

Test 3

A fellow member of your AAT local branch recently asked you for advice on report writing, and specifically on the use of appendices. Draft a short letter (making up appropriate details of your and the other person's address) explaining the purpose of an appendix, and what (s)he needs to do to ensure that (s)he uses appendices effectively. Use a fully blocked letter layout.

Test 4

The business you work for ordered five laptop computers with a list price of £500 each (order ref NCA124). During a phone conversation on 1 May 20X1 you were promised a 5% bulk discount by an account manager at the supplier (Bell computers) if you purchased five or more laptops. The account manager at the supplier is called Bill Fences.

The laptops have just arrived (20 May 20X1) and so has the invoice from the supplier (Invoice number LT241). The invoice shows the total value of the computers to be £2,500 and the 5% discount had not been deducted. You have tried phoning Bill but he is out of the office today.

You are on holiday for the rest of the week and are not going to be able to deal with this so your supervisor Hugh Martin has asked you send him a short memo explaining what happened with any photocopies of related documents attached. He will then contact the supplier to ask for a credit note and a new invoice.

Draft the memo you have been asked for.

Test 5

Write a brief email to a non-accountant explaining why the balance on a supplier's purchase ledger account might not agree to the balance on the statement sent by the supplier. You may invent appropriate email addresses, using the format firstnameinitial-surname@company.co.uk.

Test 6

Your organisation has calculated the amount of time its staff spend using email as follows.

	Accounts	Sales	Admin	Purchasing
January	80 hours	180 hours	50 hours	80 hours
February	90 hours	160 hours	80 hours	90 hours
March	105 hours	120 hours	60 hours	70 hours
April	100 hours	180 hours	70 hours	60 hours
May	110 hours	165 hours	60 hours	40 hours
June	80 hours	170 hours	50 hours	60 hours

The Accounts department has four people; Sales has five people; Admin has two people; and Purchasing has two people.

You have been asked to propose how your organisation might introduce email policies to:

(a)   prevent abuse or misuse of email by staff

(b)   make email use more efficient and effective and

(c)   protect the organisation against liability for problems caused by the abuse or misuse of email (such as the transmission of viruses, or breach of confidentiality if emails are sent to the wrong person).

Using material from this chapter and/or your own knowledge, draft a short informal report to the Accounts Manager, Mr Czwynski:

(a)   Showing (using figures and/or appropriate diagrams)

    (i)   The *total* time spent on email by each of the departments over six months (comparing their relative usage)

    (ii)   The mean average time spent on email *per month* by all departments (showing month on month trends)

    (iii)   The time spent on email *per employee* over six months, in each department

(b)   Explaining the risks and costs of abuse or misuse of email

(c)   Suggesting examples of email policies that could be implemented. Include a sample 'signature block' for external outgoing emails, as an Appendix to the report.

chapter 6:
WORKING INDEPENDENTLY

─── chapter coverage 📖 ───

In this chapter, you will develop the knowledge and skills required to plan and manage your own workload effectively. We discuss important issues in personal effectiveness such as prioritising, flexibility, confidentiality and meeting deadlines. We also examine the use of a range of planning aids and organisational tools.

This chapter explains how to prioritise and schedule tasks and to plan the use of your time: these are all tasks you could be expected to perform in the assessment. It also includes a section on the importance of meeting deadlines.

The topics covered are:

✍ What is involved in a 'job'?

✍ Time management

✍ Setting and managing priorities

✍ Planning aids

✍ Monitoring plans

✍ Meeting deadlines

✍ Adhering to working practices and policies

WHAT IS INVOLVED IN A 'JOB?'

A 'job' is a collection of tasks and responsibilities allocated to an individual. Some organisations allocate a defined set of tasks to individuals in particular positions, while others allow teams to allocate tasks among themselves more flexibly (within the constraints set by the team's goals and targets for performance).

Job description

A key element in being able to work effectively is knowing exactly what is required of you (and what you are *not* necessarily expected to do). In most cases, an employee will be given a JOB DESCRIPTION when (s)he enters a position. This should include a job title and an outline of the main tasks and responsibilities involved in the job.

You could be provided with a job description in your assessment which describes the tasks and responsibilities involved in 'your' job.

HOW IT WORKS

When you started work at Southfield Electronics, you were given the job description shown below.

JOB DESCRIPTION

Job title:	Accounts clerk, financial accounting
Location:	London office
Job summary:	General financial accounting duties
Key responsibilities	Providing administrative and clerical support to the Assistant Financial Accountants and Payroll Manager, including filing, answering the telephone and dealing with post
	Undertaking work as requested, including: obtaining quotes from suppliers; preparing daily cheque listings, sales invoices, credit notes and monthly sales summaries; and checking purchase invoices to goods received notes
	Using own initiative to deal with enquiries in the absence of the Assistant Financial Accountants
	Being aware of the importance of maintaining strict confidentiality in all aspects of work

Reporting structure:

Financial accountant
|
Assistant financial accountants (2)
and Payroll manager
|
Accounts clerk

Hours:	9.00 am to 5.30 pm Monday to Friday 1 hour for lunch
Training:	Induction training will be provided Continuing Professional Development encouraged
Prepared by:	Head of HR
Date:	March 20X0

TIME MANAGEMENT

Time is a resource – the same as money, information, materials and equipment. You have a fixed and limited amount of it, and various demands in your work (and non-work) life compete for a share of it. If you work in an organisation, your 'time is money': you will be paid for it, or for what you accomplish with it.

Time, like any other resource, needs to be managed if it is to be used efficiently (without waste) and effectively (productively).

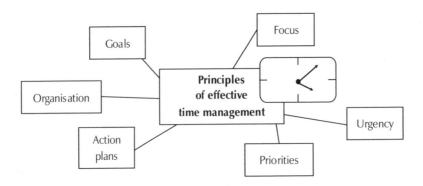

The key principles of TIME MANAGEMENT (according to *John Adair*) can be summarised as follows:

- *Set goals* for all aspects of your work, so that you know what you want to achieve – and can tell when you have done so.

- *Formulate action plans* that set out how you intend to achieve your goals: the timescale, deadlines, the tasks involved, resources required and so on. (We will look at various planning aids a later on.)

- *Set priorities*: decide which tasks are the most important – what is the most valuable use of your time at this moment? – and list them in the order in which you would tackle them. (We discuss how to do this below.)

- *Focus*: give your attention to one thing at a time, if possible. Make sure that everything you need for the task is available, avoid interruptions if you can – and then concentrate.

- *Urgency*: do not put off tasks because they are difficult or large. (They will only get worse as the deadline approaches!) Work on any task you are doing as if it were urgent.

- *Organisation*: develop positive work habits which minimise the time and effort spent (and wasted) on tasks. Do similar tasks (eg photocopying) in batches to avoid multiple trips to the photocopier. Keep your filing up-to-date, so you know where to find things. Manage your in-tray: don't let things 'pile up' without dealing with them or making a plan to do so.

Routine tasks

Much of your day at work will revolve around the carrying out of the ROUTINE TASKS that will have been summarised in your job description. Some of these will be daily tasks, such as opening the post, doing the filing and dealing with incoming emails. Other tasks may be weekly tasks, such as paying suppliers' invoices or monthly items, such as preparing the bank reconciliation statement.

HOW IT WORKS

Every day at Southfield Electronics, you are (as stated in your job description) required to open the post in the morning. You have to list any *cheques* received from customers and give the cheque listing to Kellie McDonald. If any *purchase invoices* are received from suppliers, you retain them for checking against 'goods received' documentation during the week. Once checked, you hand them over to Kellie McDonald each Friday morning for payment.

You *distribute* any other post received to the in-trays of the relevant people each morning.

During each day, you will receive *despatch notes* from the Stores department, for goods which have been sent out to customers. Each day, you are required to prepare *sales invoices* corresponding to these despatch notes, which are then sent to the financial accountant, Jenny Faulkner, for checking by the end of each day: they are then sent out to the customers the next day.

You will also receive *goods returned notes* from the Stores department. By the end of each week, you must have produced, and sent to Jenny Faulkner, a *credit note* for each goods returned note.

At the end of each month, Jenny Faulkner requires a *listing of all invoices and credit notes* sent out during the month.

A number of times per week, you will receive *purchase requisitions* which have been authorised by Jenny Faulkner. Your task is to email the appropriate suppliers, requesting *quotations*, and to prepare *purchase orders* from approved suppliers.

All copy invoices, credit notes, purchase invoices and purchase requisitions should be *filed* each day.

As office junior, you are also (informally) expected to ensure that there is tea, coffee, milk and biscuits in the office kitchen.

In order to keep track of all these routine tasks, you summarise them in a helpful format, as follows.

Daily	■ Open post
	■ Prepare cheque listing
	■ Distribute other post
	■ Check emails and respond
	■ Prepare sales invoices
	■ Filing
	■ Check kitchen supplies
Weekly	■ Check purchase orders – ready for Friday morning
	■ Send quotation requests and purchase orders
	■ Prepare credit notes
Monthly	■ Prepare sales invoice/credit note listing

Unexpected tasks

As well as the general, routine tasks that are part of your role, you may also be asked to perform non-routine or unexpected tasks. These may be one-off special jobs, cover for an employee who is off sick, or assisting a colleague to complete his or her task. They may also include the handling of enquiries or queries from customers, suppliers or other staff members.

Such tasks are part of general working life, and you will need to fit them into your work schedule. This is why the guidance notes for this Unit refer to 're-prioritising tasks within your workload': in other words, *adjusting* your plans and priorities to take account of *changing demands*.

Task 1

What is the difference between routine tasks and unexpected tasks? Give two examples of each.

Urgent tasks and important tasks

Some tasks will be URGENT TASKS: they need to be completed for a deadline *in the near future*. For example, the marketing director may request a breakdown of sales by product for a meeting first thing tomorrow morning.

Other tasks might be classified as IMPORTANT TASKS. These are jobs that have major value or potential consequences for the organisation: for example, preparing cost estimates for a major purchase, or a report for a high-level meeting. A task will be classed as important if:

- Other people or tasks *rely* on its timely completion (a task which is relatively unimportant to you may be an important part of someone else's work); and/or

- The *consequences* of non-completion are high (in terms of costs, damage, delay); and/or

- It has been requested by an individual or body which has high *power* (eg a senior manager or government agency).

It is natural to think that an urgent task is important – or that an important task is urgent – but this is not necessarily the case. You may have *time* to devote to the important task – or you may have to 'drop' an urgent task because it is not as *important* as another requirement. This is a question of *priority*.

Task 2

What is the difference between urgent tasks and important tasks? Give two examples of each.

SETTING AND MANAGING PRIORITIES

Even with routine tasks, it may be necessary to plan the *order* in which you will carry them out on a given day or week. When *unexpected* tasks are introduced as well, this form of planning becomes even more important. The process of determining the order in which tasks should be carried out is known as PRIORITISING. So how do you go about it?

Prioritising by urgency and importance

Clearly, urgent tasks are higher-priority than non-urgent tasks, and important tasks are higher-priority than unimportant tasks. You might therefore use a simple framework of four categories.

Urgent and important	Tasks that must be done in the very near future and which are important to you and to other people in the organisation. (For example, you are asked to produce a report for a manager for a high-level strategy meeting tomorrow morning.)
Not urgent but important	Tasks which are important but not immediately due. (For example, today is Monday and the project manager has asked for some product costings for Friday.) Beware, however, if you leave non-urgent tasks too long, they *become* urgent!
Urgent but not important	Tasks which are urgent – but will not be a major problem if not completed in time. (For example, there is no milk in the kitchen, and the shops are about to close. The worst that can happen is some grumbling, until you can find time to shop the following morning.)
Not urgent and not important	Tasks that can be slotted into the gaps between higher-priority tasks. (For example, periodically you may pack up out-of-date files to be stored in the archives.)

HOW IT WORKS

As well as your routine duties at Southfield Electronics (detailed earlier), you discover that a number of other tasks are required of you today, Thursday, when you come into work.

- There is no milk in the fridge, and it is your responsibility to replace it.

- Jenny Faulkner has left a note on your desk saying that she needs the November sales figures by lunchtime, for a meeting with the Managing Director.

- Kellie McDonald requires photocopies of the cheque listings for the last two weeks by Friday lunchtime.

Remember that you also have your routine duties to carry out. How should you plan your day? To start with, you could categorise your tasks according to their urgency and importance.

Category	Tasks	Comments
Urgent and important	Open and distribute post Produce daily cheque listing Check emails *Plus* November sales figures (today)	Although the routine tasks are not as important as the job for Jenny, they are still important: your colleagues rely on you completing them.
Not urgent but important	Prepare sales invoices Check purchase invoices ready (Fri) Check credit notes prepared *Plus* copy cheque listings (Fri)	There should be time to fit these in around the urgent/important tasks – but keep an eye on them, because they will *become* urgent if left too long.
Urgent but not important	Buy milk	May be important to colleagues, so perhaps persuade one of them to do you a favour (in their own interests) and go to the shop!

Your day can now be organised with the tasks undertaken in the order suggested by the above analysis.

Other prioritising techniques

If tasks are of equal urgency and importance, or there are no particular issues of priority, the following are some other possible criteria for determining the order in which tasks should be completed.

- Arrival time: performing tasks in the order in which they are requested.

- Most nearly finished: starting with the task nearest completion. (It is satisfying ticking off finished tasks – and frustrating to interrupt a nearly-complete task to start something else.)

- Shortest task first: enabling you to get lots of tasks out of the way quickly.

- Longest/most difficult task first: enabling you to get some momentum on tasks you might otherwise procrastinate over!

- Difficulty of handover: if you are about to go on holiday, say, you should tackle the things that it will be most difficult for someone else to take over while you are away.

Task 3

It is 4.00 pm on Friday afternoon and you are in the process of printing off the sales invoices for the day, to be checked by the accountant and sent out this evening. Your supervisor approaches you and asks you to print out a confidential report that she requires for a meeting on Monday at 12.00 noon. There is only one printer in the Accounts department. You estimate that there are still another 30 minutes of sales invoice printing, and that the report will take about two-and-a-half hours to print.

What should you do?

In the assessment you could be provided with a number of work requests and deadlines, which you would then have to prioritise and organise in order to ensure that they will all be completed on time.

Dealing with changes in priority

Just because you have planned your tasks for a day or a week does not mean that they are fixed in stone! As other unexpected tasks come along, you may well need to change your priorities – and therefore the order in which you carry out your jobs.

HOW IT WORKS

You have been working hard in the Financial Accounts department at Southfield Electronics this Thursday morning and by 11.30 am, you have produced the November sales figures for Jenny, opened the post, prepared the cheque listing and distributed the post. You also managed to persuade Amy Laval to go out and buy the milk. However, you are just about to check your emails when Jenny Faulkner comes over to your desk.

She tells you that Sam Piper, the new accounts assistant, has gone home ill. One of Sam's most urgent tasks today was to prepare statements for two large customers who are querying the amount that they owe. As you have done this before, Jenny asks you if you will perform this task for Sam and get the statements to her by 4.00 pm for checking and sending out in the post tonight.

You now have to change your priorities, as this task is both urgent and important. Your day will now look as follows:

- Prepare customer statements by 4.00 pm at the latest
- Check emails – deal with any that are urgent
- Photocopy the cheque listings for Kelly McDonald
- Prepare sales invoices for the day
- Check that purchase invoices will be ready for Friday morning
- Check that all credit notes have been prepared

A pretty full day!

Task 4

An accounts assistant has the following routine daily duties:

- Enter sales invoices/credit notes in computer in batches
- Enter purchase invoices/credit notes in computer in batches
- Enter cash receipts in computer
- Enter cheque payments in computer
- Print daily cheque run
- Deal with customer queries
- File all sales and purchases invoices and credit notes

Today is Thursday and there are three messages on the accounts assistant's desk when she arrives for work.

- The first is from the accountant asking for a statement to be sent to a major customer today – all post must be in the mail out-tray by 4.00 pm

- The second is from a colleague asking for the balances on the accounts of eight customers which he requires for a meeting at 10.00 am tomorrow

- The third is from the HR manager asking the accounts assistant to attend a meeting in the HR office at 3.00 pm.

How would the accounts assistant prioritise her tasks for the day?

Scheduling tasks

Once you have a list of priorities, you will need to SCHEDULE tasks, by determining *when* you will tackle them.

Determining the time that it will take to do a task is easy if it is a routine procedure that you have done many times before: simply note how long it takes you, on average. With non-routine tasks, particularly substantial ones, it can be far more difficult to determine how long to allow. You can ask someone with more experience than you, or you might be able to break the task down into smaller stages whose duration you can more easily estimate. The important thing is to be realistic!

Time schedules can be determined by different methods.

- Forward scheduling: *adding* the estimated duration of each task from its scheduled *starting* time/date, to give you the target completion time/date. This is useful for scheduling routine tasks.

- Backward scheduling: *subtracting* the estimated duration of each task from its *deadline* or completion time/date. This gives you the latest start from which you'll get the job done in time – so schedule an earlier start where possible! This method is useful for meeting deadlines and for complex tasks, where each stage depends on the timely completion of the previous stage.

- Slotting your tasks into appropriate start dates/times, in order of priority – and fitting lower-priority tasks around higher-priority ones. Remember to check that your daily schedule only adds up to the number of working hours in your day (allowing for lunch breaks, routine daily jobs and scheduled meetings!) Tasks which don't 'fit' can then be moved to a bigger 'slot' (if they have to be done all in one go) or carried over for completion on another day.

Protecting your time

In addition to *planning* your time, time management requires you to *control* – and sometimes *protect* – your time, in the face of changing and competing demands.

- You may need to *delegate* less important tasks which can be done by other people, in order to free up your time for more important tasks which only you can do.

- You may need to develop skills in *assertiveness* (stating clearly, firmly but calmly what you feel, need or want), in order to ask for help when you need it – or to say 'no' when others inappropriately make demands on your time.

We look at this, in the context of working as part of a team, in Chapter 7, but it is important to remember that if a colleague or manager tries to add something to your planned and agreed schedule, this may cause a *conflict of priorities*, and you will have to negotiate solutions to such conflicts. As we have seen, the solution may be to re-prioritise your schedule, if it is flexible enough, or to ask for assistance or extra time where necessary.

However, it may be that the only solution is to say 'no' to requests, if they are unreasonable. In a professional setting – and particularly if the requester is in a position of authority – this will have to be done courteously and positively (proposing alternative ways of getting their demands met if possible), but also firmly.

PLANNING AIDS

There is a wide variety of PLANNING AIDS that can help you to ensure that all of your tasks are remembered, scheduled, monitored and completed on time.

To Do List

The simplest planning aid is a 'To Do List', tick list or checklist. Here you simply write down each task that is required of you for the day, preferably in prioritised order. Then as each task is completed, you tick it off from the list – the satisfying part!

At the end of the day, anything left un-ticked on the To Do list can be carried over to tomorrow's To Do list and fitted into tomorrow's tasks and priorities.

Another advantage of this technique is that, if you have to hand your tasks over to someone else, it is easy for them to see where you are 'up to'.

Diary or timetable

The purpose of the diary or timetable is to slot events, tasks or meetings into clearly labelled time 'slots' (hours or days), where they become an easily used reminder (and signal that that time is 'taken' and cannot be used for other scheduled items).

Diaries also offer a useful follow-up system, because you can schedule questions, checks and follow-up actions: for example, to check that you have received the data you requested on the day it was due.

Diaries and timetables can be paper-based or electronic (eg using a PDA, electronic personal organiser, mobile phone or computer). Software such as Microsoft Outlook and Palm Desktop is often used to combine a diary, alarm clock (notifying you of the time for diarised events), To Do list (with reminders as you approach deadlines) and address book (in case you need to contact other people involved).

You might like to experiment with such tools if you have access to them. The limitations of such systems are: they do not guarantee efficient or organised working; it is easy to grow dependent on them (to the point where loss or damage creates chaos); and they can take quite a lot of time to use effectively!

Planning schedules and charts

Schedules and charts are often used for more complex tasks or projects. They tend to be used when a project involves a number of separate tasks, some of which must be completed before others can be started. Longer-term planning schedules may be conveniently set out using charts or monthly/yearly 'planners'.

Bar charts are often used to 'block out' periods of time on a calendar, to show when tasks are scheduled, or when staff members are on holiday. This has the advantage of clearly showing where tasks fall in the month/year, what order they fall in, where they overlap and so on.

A *PLANNING SCHEDULE* is a form of bar chart, but each division of space represents both an amount of time and an amount of work to be done in that time. Lines or bars drawn across the space indicate how much work is scheduled to be done and/or how much work has actually been done.

This makes it easy to measure your progress, and whether you are ahead of schedule or behind schedule. Here's an example of a planning schedule for a small furniture maker, showing work in progress against schedule at the morning break time on Thursday 8th March 20X0.

Job	Mon 5	Tue 6	Wed 7	Thur 8	Fri 9	Mon 12	Tue 13
Table							
Shelves							
Kitchen units							
Bed							

☐ Scheduled activity time   ■ Actual progress   ✼ Time now

Task 5

What can you tell from this planning chart about the furniture maker's progress on the scheduled tasks for the week?

HOW IT WORKS

Management accountant, Kate Saltmarsh, has to produce the quarterly cost accounts for the quarter ending 30 November for the Finance Director by Monday 13 December. From experience she knows the following.

- Once she has all of the information to hand, it will take her two full days (around her other tasks) to produce the accounts.

- She will need a variety of information from the assistant management accountants and this will take them two days to prepare.

- The typing of the accounts can be done in half a day and then there will be another half day of proofing and checking.

- The accounts must be sent to the general office for binding which will take a further day.

If Kate is to have the accounts on the Finance Director's desk by the morning of Monday 13, she will have to start work some time in advance. So she draws up a To Do List, *backward scheduling* based on having the accounts fully bound at close of business on Friday 10 December.

> **To Do List**
>
> - Friday 10 December – binding
> - Thursday 9 December – typing and proofing
> - Tuesday 7 and Wednesday 8 December – preparation time
> - Friday 3 December – request information from assistants

Kate then realises that she will be out of the office all day on Tuesday 7 December, and will need to allow for this as well. The final planning schedule for the preparation of the cost accounts will therefore be as follows.

	December						
	Thur 2	Fri 3	Mon 6	Tues 7	Wed 8	Thurs 9	Fri 10
Request information	■■						
Preparation of accounts			■■		■■		
Typing and proofing						■■	
Binding							■■

From this Kate will also be able to warn the typist to be ready for the work on Thursday 9 December, and warn the general office to be ready for the binding task on Friday 10 December.

Task 6

At the end of Friday 5 October, your in-tray includes a number of work requests for the following week. You collate them to draw up a To Do List. (The 'job codes' are the initials of the person who requested each task, plus a number, so that you can slot them into a timetable more easily.)

Job code	Task	Approx time	Deadline (end of:)
AB1	Project cost analysis	7 hours	Wed 10th
AB2	Depreciation figures	5 hours	Wed 10th
AB3	Presentation slides	8 hours	Thurs 11th
AB4	Check inventory (stock) figures	12 hours	Mon 15th
Train	Training course	6 hours	Fri 12th: 8 am – 3 pm
AB5	Collect staff CPD plans	2 hours	Fri 26th
CD1	Check statements	6 hours	Tues 9th
EF1	Aged receivables (debtors)	6 hours	Tues 9th
EF2	Bank reconciliations	4 hours	Mon 8th

(a) Complete the timetable below, indicating what task you will work on for each hour of each working day. (Note that overtime has been authorised for a maximum of two hours each day.)

(b) Identify any task(s) where you may have difficulty meeting the deadline.

TIMETABLE					
	Mon 8	Tues 9	Wed 10	Thurs 11	Fri 12
[8.00 – 9.00]					
9.00 – 10.00					
10.00 – 11.00					
11.00 – 12.00					
12.00 – 13.00					
13.00 – 14.00					
14.00 – 15.00					
15.00 – 16.00					
16.00 – 17.00					
[17.00 – 18.00]					

Task(s) carried over to week beginning 15 October:

-
-
-

Action plans

An ACTION PLAN is an even more detailed planning tool which can be used for complex and usually longer term projects. It contains a considerable amount of detail and is monitored on a regular basis to ensure that things are going to plan and, if they are not, to devise how the situation can be rectified. An action plan normally contains:

- Details of each task which is part of the project
- Start date of each task
- Completion date for each task
- Person responsible for each task
- (In some cases) expected and actual costs

MONITORING PLANS

Plans are all well and good – but things do not always 'go to plan'! It is important that schedules are monitored to ensure that everything is happening as and when expected. If not, adjustments may have to be made *either* to how the task is being done (if extra effort or resources are required) – *or* to the plan or deadline (if it was unrealistic, say).

All individuals must maintain checks and controls over their work, to ensure that stages of work are 'on track', that jobs have in fact been completed at the deadline (or payments made when they fall due), and that agreed follow-up actions are not forgotten.

Checklists are useful for monitoring what has been done and what hasn't. *Diary systems* may also be used. Some computer-based organiser systems issue alert messages when the scheduled event or completion time approaches.

You should keep copies of work plans and schedules, and any work request forms (or other communications in which you are asked to perform tasks). This will enable you to:

- Check that your work is on track with your current schedule

- Review and keep track of original work requests, plans and priorities, as the situation changes

- Monitor the need for follow-up action

- Review your scheduling and workload management, perhaps with your supervisor or learning coach, to see how effectively you have translated work requests into plans and schedules.

MEETING DEADLINES

A DEADLINE is a set or agreed time when a task must be completed. It is important to realise that deadlines are set for a reason. Some are obvious reasons: the sales director has a meeting with a large customer this afternoon, say, and needs a printout of the sales to this customer for the last six months. The time of the meeting is the (obvious) deadline.

Other reasons for deadlines may not be so obvious. Your line manager has asked for some figures for Wednesday, because she has to write a report for Monday morning: you don't necessarily know that it will take her two days to complete the report – but she does.

Missing deadlines

If you fail to complete the task by the deadline, this will affect the person who has asked you to undertake the work – and has then relied on you to do so.

There may be occasions when it will become apparent that you are going to struggle to meet a deadline. This could be for a number of reasons.

- Your workload may be too great for you to finish on time.

- Colleagues who are providing you with required information may have failed to meet their deadlines for doing so.

- You may not have planned effectively or worked efficiently enough.

- Unexpected, higher-priority demands may have been placed on your time, pushing lower-priority tasks back.

Reporting problems in meeting deadlines

Whatever the reason, if you become aware that you may not meet a deadline you must report the fact immediately to the appropriate person. This may be the individual who has requested the work, your supervisor or line manager, or a colleague who is relying on the work.

It is never easy to admit to someone that you are not able to complete a task on time, but it is important that you do so *as soon as you anticipate difficulties.*

- The person expecting the work may find that if you miss your deadline, they will miss theirs – and they will need time to adjust their plans or warn others.

- A manager may be able to take action to enable you to meet your deadline.

This second point is particularly important. Provided that you report any anticipated difficulties in meeting a deadline early enough, there are actions that can be taken to help! The manager can:

- Put pressure on any other employees who are holding you up by not producing the information you require.

- Lighten your existing workload in order to free up time to meet the deadline.

- Provide you with additional resources, such as extra computer time or another colleague's time.

- Adjust plans, so that you will have more time.

Task 7

If you think that you will not be able to meet a deadline, why is it important to report this to the appropriate person immediately?

Seeking assistance with problems

The first stage is to *recognise* that you are not going to be able to complete the assignment without some additional help. Be prepared to admit this to yourself, if necessary!

When you ask for assistance, try to *identify* what resources you require: extra time to get the task done yourself, say – or additional computer time or help from a colleague.

If you are in a position to delegate work to more junior team members, they may provide the extra resources required. However, in many cases you will have to approach a more senior manager or colleagues and *request* assistance. You will need to explain *why* you need the assistance and *what* you think is required. You may need to *negotiate*: persuading the other person to help you, by showing how it will benefit them, or by offering something they want in return.

Once you have been granted assistance, it is important that it is in fact a help – not a hindrance! Helpers need to be properly briefed on what is required. At the same time, assisting you should not become a burden or disruption to the other person's work.

It may be that your assessment will include information indicating that you have been asked to carry out a task and that you are unable to complete it by the required deadline. You will be expected to identify this and explain the action you would take.

ADHERING TO WORKING PRACTICES AND POLICIES

We discussed some of the legal, policy and procedural requirements for accounting and payroll – and why it is important to adhere to them – in Chapters 2 and 3.

It is important to adhere to *any* agreed working practice, even if it is just 'customary', because other people will be basing their plans and conduct on their expectation that you will do so. If you depart from accepted procedures and practices, you are creating a risk of disruption to plans and damage to working relationships – as well as, perhaps, risks to health and safety, confidentiality, the integrity of data and so on: all the things the procedures and practices are designed to protect.

Communicating with your line manager or supervisor

In general, you will need to adhere to instructions and departmental practices for maintaining communication with your supervisor or line manager, in a range of situations including:

- Providing information, and reporting on work progress and results, where this is routine or requested

- Reporting by exception: that is, reporting when there has been some deviation or variance from the plan or budget

- Seeking advice and assistance for decisions or actions beyond your competence to perform effectively

- Seeking authorisation for decisions or actions beyond the scope of your authority to deal with

- Receiving information and instructions, perhaps as part of regular or occasional team briefings

- Seeking and receiving feedback on your work performance

- Seeking learning and development opportunities in your work, eg if your supervisor is willing to act as an on-the-job coach, or has responsibility for authorising your development objectives and plans.

You will need to observe established customs and protocols for how this communication takes place. Your manager may exercise informal 'management by walking around'; you may have defined opportunities for communication (eg in regular meetings, briefings or 'open door' hours); or you may need to put information and queries in writing, using email or memoranda.

Organising and maintaining your own work area

As we mentioned in Chapter 3, the maintenance of your work area is often the subject of organisational policies, mainly aimed at ensuring that offices maintain a professional image, and reflect the corporate image of the organisation, particularly in areas which are visited by outsiders.

However, it is also your responsibility to organise your work area so that it helps with – and does not interfere with – efficient and effective work habits. This might mean:

- Positioning your desk (where possible) to ensure that you have sufficient space for your activities

- Ensuring that you and others can move efficiently and safely around the work area, without obstructions or hazards

- Positioning chairs for visitors, printer tables and filing cabinets for efficient use

- Organising your desk top and shelving to ensure that items you use regularly are within reach – and that your space is generally tidy, so that you and others can easily find items when required. Aids to organisation include: document trays, desktop organisers, devices to keep electrical wiring out of the way, pin boards (where you can stick reminders etc) and filing systems

- Ensuring that you tidy away all sensitive and confidential documents (and their computer equivalents) when you leave your desk unattended, and especially when you leave work at the end of the day, in order to protect the security of the data.

Respecting confidentiality

We covered the need for confidentiality (and data security) in Chapter 3, but it is always worth repeating! In order to work effectively in accounting and finance, you must be aware of – and adhere to – all work practices and procedures involving rules of disclosure and non-disclosure, the protection of confidentiality, and the secure handling and storage of sensitive data.

CHAPTER OVERVIEW

- An employee's job will usually consist of a variety of tasks which may be set out in a job, role or competence description.

- A typical job will be made up of a number of daily/weekly/monthly routine tasks plus other unexpected tasks to which schedules must be adapted as required.

- Tasks can be categorised as urgent or non-urgent and important or unimportant when setting priorities.

- You must be able to deal with changes in priorities and therefore changes to your planned work schedule.

- A variety of planning aids can be used to ensure that all tasks are completed on time: eg To Do lists, diaries or timetables, planning schedules and action plans.

- If it appears that a deadline may not be met, it is important to report the difficulty to the appropriate person as soon as possible, and to negotiate assistance where possible.

- Time management is a combination of effective work planning and control of time (eg through delegation and assertiveness).

- Legal and policy constraints apply to your working practices in areas such as maintaining your own work area and respecting confidentiality. (Recap your learning from Chapter 2 if you need to.)

Keywords

Job description – a written summary of the main duties and tasks required as part of a particular job

Time management – ensuring that work is carried out efficiently and effectively, so that all tasks are completed on time and within the time available

Routine tasks – the general daily, weekly, monthly tasks which make up a job

Urgent tasks – tasks for which there is a deadline in the near future

Important tasks – tasks which affect other people or outcomes; on which others depend; or which have significant (positive or negative) impact

Prioritising – ordering tasks according to their degree of urgency and importance

Schedule – the allocation of tasks to appropriate times/dates when they will be tackled or completed

Planning aids – tools, formats and techniques for organising tasks and projects

Action plan – detailed record of all of the tasks involved in a complex project – normally including start and finish dates and responsibility for each task

Deadline – a set time when a task must be completed

TEST YOUR LEARNING

Test 1

If you prioritise your tasks for a day on the basis of whether or not they are urgent and whether or not they are important, there would be four categories of tasks. What are these four categories, and what order should you carry them out? Give an example of a typical task that might fall into each category.

Test 2

An accounts assistant has the following routine duties:

- Open the morning post
- Pass any cheques received to the cashier
- Deal with emails
- Deal with any employee petty cash claims
- Enter sales invoices/credit notes daily in batches into computer system
- Match purchase invoices to goods received notes daily and pass to the accountant for authorisation
- File sales invoices/credit notes daily
- File paid purchase invoices weekly every Friday

Today is Friday 27 September and having opened the post and passed the cheques to the cashier, you get a telephone call from the accountant to say that one of your colleagues is not coming in today due to sickness.

You now also need to enter the weekly purchase invoices into the computer before the end of the day. You also have a pile of about 20 purchase invoices that need to be matched to GRNs before the end of the day.

It is now 10.30 am. In what order would you carry out these tasks (assuming that no employees need to have petty cash claims dealt with yet)?

Test 3

Continuing from the previous task: following your lunch break you return to your desk at 1.30 pm. You have already entered the sales invoices, credit notes and purchase invoices into the computer system, so you are fairly relaxed about the rest of your day. However there are two notes on your desk when you return from lunch.

Please can I have a summary of the petty cash book for the last month, for a meeting first thing on Monday morning? *Thanks.* *Accountant*	*Please call Harry Featherstone, salesman. He has an urgent petty cash claim that he needs to make.*

You call Harry Featherstone and arrange for him to come in to see you at 2.30 pm. You estimate that the petty cash summary will take an hour-and-a-half and you must leave the office at 5.30 pm this evening.

How would you schedule your afternoon?

Test 4

You have been asked to prepare a report on the payment patterns of twelve of your organisation's largest customers. The information for the current month will not be available until Tuesday 5 April. However, the information for earlier months is to be collated by a colleague and she thinks that this will take her two days. The report should take you about four days to prepare on your computer around your other tasks. You should be able to work for two days without the current month information. Six copies of the report are required for a Board meeting on Friday 8 March at 2.00 pm. You estimate that it will take three hours to print and collate the copies of the report.

Prepare a planning schedule for production of this report.

Test 5

Describe an action plan and list the information it normally includes. Contrast it with a 'To Do List'.

Test 6

You have been asked to prepare a report for your manager which must be with her on Wednesday 22 August. You will need to requisition some files for this, which will take a day to arrive. You estimate that the research will take you three days and the analysis required another two days. The report will be with the typist for a further day and then you will need one final day for checking and proofing.

(a) Using whatever planning aids you think appropriate, schedule the preparation of this report.

(b) The day before the report is due to be typed, you check with the typist to ensure that she is expecting the job, but she apologises and says that due to her being off sick for a day the previous week, the earliest that she can start the job is Tuesday 21st. What should you do?

Test 7

Write an email to your new colleague Nasif Hassem, explaining:

(a) Why it is important to meet any deadlines set for a task in the Accounts department

(b) What staff members should do if they believe they cannot meet a specific deadline.

EMAIL	
To:	n.hassem@hazchem.com
From:	y.name@hazchem.com
Date:	
Subject:	

Test 8

Your name is Justine Spring and you have recently been employed as an accounts assistant by Reeves Ltd, a company which produces and sells a variety of educational children's toys.

The job description below was given to you when you joined the company and was discussed with the HR manager. From it, list your daily, weekly and monthly routine tasks.

JOB DESCRIPTION	
Job title:	Accounts assistant
Summary:	General financial and management accounting duties
Job content:	Enter daily sales invoices into computer
	Enter daily cash/cheque receipts into computer
	Enter daily cash/cheque payments into computer
	Prepare monthly bank reconciliation
	Deal with daily petty cash claims
	Enter petty cash details in computer weekly
	Assist in preparation of weekly payroll
	Other ad hoc financial/management accounting tasks
Reports to:	Accountant – Patrick Fellows
Hours:	9.00 am to 5.30 pm Monday to Friday
	1 hour for lunch
Training:	Necessary training to be provided
Prepared by:	HR manager

Test 9

On Friday 27 February 20X9, you arrive at work knowing that you have your routine sales invoice entries to make in the computer (normally takes about two hours); cash/cheque receipts and payments to enter into the computer (normally takes about two hours), petty cash claims to deal with (normally only about 30 minutes per day). You also have the monthly bank reconciliation which normally takes about two hours and must be completed by 5.00 pm. The petty cash entries to the computer should also be made today (normally about one hour) but these can be postponed until Monday. The cash/cheque receipts and payments for the day must be entered into the computer before the bank reconciliation can be completed but the sales invoice entries can be put off until Monday.

When you arrive at your desk you find the following additional work:

- The accountant has asked you for a list of invoices sent out to a particular customer for a meeting at 1.00 pm today. You estimate that this will take you about one hour to compile.

- The HR manager has left a message warning you that at the end of the sales conference this afternoon, at about 3.00 pm, most of the sales representatives will come to you for their petty cash claims to be processed. You anticipate that this will take a further 30 minutes of your time on top of the normal petty cash claims for the day.

Determine the order in which you would perform the tasks required of you for the day. Briefly explain why you have prioritised the tasks in the way that you have.

Test 10

For a three-week period, as part of the Personal Development Plan agreed at your last performance appraisal with the accounts supervisor, Mrs Tancredi, you have been seconded to a Task Force auditing your organisation's data security practices. The head of the task force is the IT manager, Mr Sproule. You have been given a work area in the IT department, and your routine accounting duties have been re-allocated for the next three weeks.

It is coming up to the end of week two of your secondment, and you are aware that you are going to have problems completing your report on the employee database, as agreed, by the end of week three. You are having trouble obtaining the information you require from the HR assistant, Jenny Gomez. Jenny is unable to say when she will have time to prepare your data – but without it, you can go no further in preparing your report.

Meanwhile, your colleague, Parvinder, in the Accounts department, who has been covering your routine accounting duties, is due to go on his annual holiday the day after you return to the department, giving him a day to brief you on what has been going on and what tasks are as yet unfinished.

(a) Outline your problem in this scenario, and what its effects might be.
(b) Whom do you need to inform, and of what?
(c) Draft a brief memo to the first person you need to inform.

chapter 7:
WORKING AS PART OF A TEAM

chapter coverage 📖

In this chapter we consider the benefits and problems of working as part of a team, and how you can best contribute to efficient and effective team working.

We also consider the problem of conflicts and dissatisfactions within your work role and environment, and how they can be resolved.

The topics covered are:

✍ The nature of teams and team working

✍ Working as part of a team

✍ The impact of your work on colleagues

✍ Conflict and dissatisfaction at work

✍ Resolving conflicts and dissatisfactions

TEAMS AND TEAM WORKING

In most work situations, you will find that you are not working in isolation, but as part of a work group. This work group might be a department such as the Accounts department, or a section of a department such as the Payroll section. If this group works closely together, and has a strong sense of shared goals and identity, it may be thought of as a TEAM.

A team is a small number of people with complementary skills who are committed to a common purpose, performance goals and approach, for which they hold themselves jointly accountable.

People working together in organisations need to recognise their mutual obligations to each other, and their shared tasks and objectives. They need to recognise their roles and relationships with respect to each other, as determined by their position and function in the team and in the organisation. They need to treat each other with mutual respect, within guidelines of acceptable and professional behaviour. They need to resolve any differences and conflicts that may reduce personal and team effectiveness. That's what team working is all about.

Advantages of team working

There are a number of advantages to working as part of a team rather than on an individual basis.

- *Additional resources*: a team provides extra skills, information, ideas and work hours, compared with working on your own

- *Inspiration*: teams are particularly useful for generating ideas and solving problems, because different people's ideas and viewpoints can influence the work and thinking of others

- *Motivation*: the shared efforts of a team and the help and support of its members can often provide additional motivation and satisfaction to team members in their work

- *Communication*: team working is a great way to get people talking about how their tasks depend on each other, and how they can work together to solve problems. Teams are a key tool for CO-ORDINATION in organisations, especially where team members (for a project, say) are drawn from different functions or units, so that there is plenty of lateral or cross-functional communication

- *SYNERGY:* for all the above reasons, teams can often accomplish more than the same individuals working alone. The concept of synergy describes how sometimes, two heads are not just better than one: they are better than two! When people work together effectively, $2 + 2 = 5$.

The downside of team working

Team working is often not easy! Individuals have different skills, personalities and working styles, and although this can contribute to team ideas and decisions, it can also cause frictions and conflicts within the team. Conflicts and disagreements (as we see later) can get in the way of effective team performance.

Some other disadvantages of team working are that decision-making takes longer (because of the need to take different views into account) and the process of working together and maintaining good relationships can actually distract team members from the task at hand.

WORKING AS PART OF A TEAM

Effective team working requires a number of elements:

- A mix and balance of people in the team
- Clear shared objectives and performance feedback
- Co-ordination, collaboration and communication

Team members

In order for a team to function well together, and to fulfil its task objectives, it needs to have a mix and balance of:

- Required skills, experience and knowledge, which people can *contribute to the task*. Different people will have varying strengths and weaknesses: team working helps to even this out – and fill any gaps!

- The way people *contribute to the functioning of the team*. These are sometimes called 'team roles'. Some members will be leaders; some 'ideas' people; others will be better at implementing or following through the ideas; still others will be the ones who help team discussion along and act as peacemakers if there is conflict. All these roles are needed in a well functioning team.

It is important for you to identify your own role in the team's performance and maintenance. What does the team need you to do, competently and reliably, in order to achieve its objectives? What does the team need you to contribute, in order to maintain effective team working?

Do not underestimate the importance of small contributions to good working relationships, like replenishing the biscuit tin, or offering support to a colleague. Conversely, do not underestimate the *negative* affect on team working of letting conflicts fester, failing to 'pull your weight' in the team, or failing to honour your commitments to other team members.

Objectives and feedback

In order for a team to work well, it must have a well-defined and well-understood purpose and objectives, which apply to all its members. This ensures that all members are working towards the same goals. Each member should have clearly set out (or jointly agreed) responsibilities – but essentially, the focus is less on individual achievement than on contributing to *group* achievement.

In some cases, the objectives of a team will be set for it by the nature of its work, and the team leader's goals for how the work should be carried out.

However, where a new team has been set up for a task or project, it may be necessary to negotiate and jointly agree objectives, targets and standards for the team.

The team will require regular feedback: information on its progress and results, so that it can learn, correct or adjust its performance – or celebrate its successes.

Task 1

Give examples from an accounts department of the 'standing' or routine objectives the department may have set for it. What other sorts of targets and standards are likely to be set?

Collaboration, co-ordination and communication

Team working is about collaboration (working together) and co-ordination (making sure that each member's work 'fits' with the work of others and contributes to the team's objectives). The key point is that the work that *you* do impacts upon the work of other people: positively or negatively!

Information that you provide will be used by other members of the team. They may not be able to complete their tasks until you have completed yours. Therefore, schedules and working methods must be set by the team leader – or by negotiation among the group – to ensure that the work of all members is co-ordinated and integrated.

As we saw in Chapter 6, it is always important to meet deadlines and commitments: within a team, it is even more important that each individual fulfils his or her responsibilities, according to agreed schedules and working practices, in order for the team to achieve its objectives.

If any team member anticipates trouble meeting his or her commitments, (s)he must inform the team leader and affected colleagues, and work with them to devise options to resolve the situation.

In general, the more communication between team members – and between the team and its leader – the more effective its performance will be. Among other things, this means that conflicts between team members must be resolved, so that they don't interfere with communication.

HOW IT WORKS

A few months into your time at Southfield Electronics, you are asked by Jenny Faulkner, the financial accountant, to form a small project team with Amy Laval (accounts clerk), Sam Piper (the new accounts clerk), Kellie McDonald (assistant financial accountant) and John Yeo (sales manager).

This morning, Friday 3 March, you, Amy, Sam, Kellie and John had a meeting with Jenny to discuss the purpose of the project team and the work that is to be done.

Jenny explained that the company is looking into changing its credit terms to credit customers and, in particular, is reviewing its policy of offering prompt payment discounts to some customers. This will require a wide-ranging analysis of credit sales, and the payment patterns of all credit customers, in order to forecast the effect of the change of policy on sales. Jenny handed out the following briefing notes.

CREDIT SALES PROJECT: BRIEFING NOTES

OBJECTIVE

Analysis of credit limits and payment patterns of all credit customers – to be produced by Kellie McDonald by Friday 31 March.

TASKS

Accounts clerks to analyse each credit customer's account for the last year. Analysis to be prepared as follows:

- Credit limit

- Number of times credit limit exceeded

- Average amount by which credit limit exceeded

- Total credit sales for the year

- If prompt payment discount offered, percentage of total credit sales on which discount is taken

- Monthly average of outstanding amount which has been due for more than 60 days and more than 90 days

[Your Name] – credit customers from A to G
Amy Laval – credit customers from H to N
Sam Piper – credit customers from O to Z

[Your Name] is also to set up a computer spreadsheet for the analysed data. Amy Laval and Sam Piper are to input the data to the spreadsheet. Kellie McDonald is to write the final report summarising the findings regarding credit limits and payment patterns, with comments on key findings by John Yeo, where relevant.

RESOURCES

Computerised receivables ledger (sales ledger)
Monthly aged receivables (debtors) listing
Manual customer data file

TIMETABLE

Computer spreadsheet to be completed by Friday 10 March

Accounts assistants' analysis to be completed by Monday 20 March

Completed spreadsheet to Kellie McDonald by Friday 24 March

You realise that, given your existing workload, you cannot possibly set up the spreadsheet and analyse all of your assigned credit customers by the due dates. You voice this concern to Jenny, and explain that you will also need test data to be input into the spreadsheet.

Jenny agrees that perhaps this is asking too much and assigns customers beginning with E and F to Amy and customers beginning with G to Sam, leaving you with a more manageable workload. Jenny also decides that Sam should have the analysis for 30 credit customers ready for you to input as test data on 13 March.

Kellie agrees to supervise the analysis and sets up a weekly meeting every Friday morning at 10.00 am in order to assess the team's progress.

THE IMPACT OF YOUR WORK ON COLLEAGUES

Members of an accounting section are generally *interdependent:* their work objectives and outputs are often linked to each other. This is even more evident in fully team-based activities and projects, where tasks, or components or stages of tasks, are shared among team members. The outputs of one person's activity will become the inputs to another's.

The most important aspect of this is that if one team member fails to complete his/her allotted/agreed tasks, or fails to complete them on time, there will be an impact on other team members and their work.

Task 2

From the learning you have already completed in Chapter 6, explain THREE impacts on a team of one member failing to meet an agreed deadline for project work.

Deadlines

We covered the importance of meeting departmental deadlines, and what to do if you encounter problems in meeting deadlines, in Chapter 6. There, we were looking at deadlines faced when working independently – but we emphasised that your work is almost always intended for use by someone else, who may rely on its timely completion. The same thing applies in team working – only more so, because of the need to co-ordinate the work of more than one person.

Refresh your memory about the importance of meeting deadlines, and what to do if you encounter problems, if you need to, by re-reading the relevant section of Chapter 6.

Mutual assistance and support

There will undoubtedly be occasions when a team member realises that (s)he cannot fulfil a work commitment, because the schedule turns out to be unrealistic, or because unforeseen factors have created a lack of time or resources.

On such occasions, other members of the team should be prepared to provide assistance or support, as required. For example, if one team member is running out of time to carry out a task, another could offer to help (if she has extra time available) or could allow the person struggling to have first option on equipment time, say. Provided that it does not impact negatively on your own work, or become a recurring pattern, 'doing a colleague a favour' can contribute to good working relationships and team performance.

In some cases, support will be personal as well as practical. Team members may support each other when they are struggling, through empathetic listening, collaborative problem-solving, encouragement, constructive feedback and so on.

HOW IT WORKS

Let's return to the Southfield Electronics credit sales project. On 10 March at 10.00 am, the first project progress meeting is held. You report that you have the spreadsheet set up and are ready for the test data to be input on Monday. Kellie checks with Sam to ensure that the test data will be ready by Monday morning. Unfortunately, Sam has to admit that he is struggling with the analysis so far and has only analysed data for 18 customers: he asks for assistance. Kellie asks you and Amy about your workloads.

You feel that you have to get on with your analysis of credit customers, as your time has been taken up by the spreadsheet. Amy also feels that in order to meet the deadline of 20 March for her analysis, she has no spare time. However, as Amy has already completed analysis of 29 customers, she suggests that the remaining 12 analyses required for the test data are simply taken from her customers. Kellie agrees and it is further agreed that you will input the test data on Monday as originally planned.

Task 3

On Monday 22 March 20X0, you are asked to take part in a team project that will take about one month – as well as your normal tasks for the financial accounts section. The team is to provide detailed costings for a new line of children's toys. It is made up of three accounts assistants (including you), a senior accounts assistant and the team leader (the cost accountant). The costings must be ready for the monthly Board meeting on Wednesday 21 April.

On Tuesday 6 April, at the weekly project team meeting, one of the other accounts assistants timidly admits that she had forgotten that the following weekend was the Easter holiday: she will not be able to meet her stage deadline. She believes that she can analyse the figures by the next day, but will not have time to input them to the computer on Thursday, the last working day of the week.

You know that you are likely to have some spare time on Thursday, as you are ahead with your routine tasks and have already completed your project tasks. What should you do in this situation and why?

Being appropriately assertive

As we mentioned in Chapter 6, it is important to *protect* your time and scheduled priorities – in order to avoid having them disrupted by the demands of other team members.

Your ability to do this, and what course of action is appropriate in a given situation, depends on a number of factors. You will need to consider:

- The authority of the person making an unexpected demand on your time. Does this person have the 'right' to ask you?

- The nature of the request: is it appropriate and reasonable, and in the best interests of the effectiveness and efficiency of the department – or can you propose a better course of action?

- The impact on other people and tasks, if you go ahead with the demand: for example, will it prevent you from meeting other deadlines?

- Which of the people making conflicting demands on you has the most authority? If they have equal authority, you might be able to ask them to negotiate a compromise between them – or you may have to refer the matter upwards to a higher authority for a decision.

- What is the most courteous, respectful, professional and assertive way to resolve the problem – without inappropriately sacrificing your own needs and interests?

ASSERTIVE COMMUNICATION means standing up for your own rights, needs and opinions (ie not being passive or a 'doormat') – *without* dismissing the rights, needs or opinions of others (ie not being 'aggressive').

You have a right to say 'no' to inappropriate or unreasonable demands – but you can choose to do this in a way that is calm, courteous, professional, positive and co-operative. The key is to state clearly and directly what the problem is, and what you want or do not want to happen. If possible, explain why you cannot comply with a demand because of its impact on your work or the interests of the team: this should defuse any suspicion that you are just being 'selfish'! You might then be able to propose alternative solutions to meet the other person's needs (can you perform their task later, or get the assistance you need to fit it in, or propose someone better placed to do it than you?) – or invite them to make alternative suggestions, which you will consider positively.

HOW IT WORKS

Back at the Southfield Electronics credit sales project, it is now the end of the day on Wednesday 22 March. You are finalising the spreadsheets for Kellie McDonald, ready to submit them to her, as requested, on Friday.

Just as you are packing up for the day, Ron Howard, another of the assistant financial accounts to whom you report, comes and asks you to do a task for him first thing tomorrow. He estimates it will take you about half a day – and it will enable him to take the morning off to take his wife to the doctor.

You are aware that you do not have half a day to spare, if you are to complete your spreadsheet work for the project. So you say, calmly and courteously to Ron:

'I'm sorry, Ron, but I have an important deadline coming up on the credit sales project. I simply don't have any time to spare tomorrow. I would love to be able to help you out – but if I don't get the spreadsheet done, Kellie and John Yeo will not have time to work on their final report.'

Ron says loudly that his work should take equal priority to Kellie's – particularly since it is genuine Accounts department work, 'not some project thing'. Obviously, you cannot take this view, since you have agreed your schedule with Kellie, who has equal authority to Ron – and also the backing of Jenny Faulkner.

Without backing down, you continue to calmly offer constructive options, suggesting that if Ron were to speak to Kellie and explain the situation, she might be able to stretch your project deadline a little – or one of the other accounts clerks might be able to help him.

Task 4

How effectively have you handled the situation in the 'How It Works' scenario above? What are the key points of the argument you make for protecting your time in this scenario?

CONFLICT AND DISSATISFACTION AT WORK

CONFLICT is the clash of opposing 'forces' – including the personalities, interests and attitudes of individuals and groups. In any working relationship or team, there are bound to be disagreements and conflicts of various kinds. There are also likely to be times when you are dissatisfied with something at work: for example, unresolved problems, frustrations, poor working conditions or unfair treatment.

Your aim in the workplace is to be able to handle disagreements, conflicts and dissatisfactions constructively, so that you can maintain good working relations and efficient individual and team working.

Causes and types of conflict

In any working relationship or team, there are bound to be conflicts on occasion. Such conflicts may be due to:

- Differences in personality (eg an outgoing person irritating a quiet, reflective person)

- Differences in working style (eg if one person likes to plan ahead and the other doesn't)

- Differences in status (eg if team members feel powerless or micro-managed by a powerful boss, or unable to raise problems because a manager is seen as 'unapproachable')

- The interdependency of work (eg if one person or team is frustrated by delays caused by another's missed deadline, or someone within the team isn't 'pulling their weight' and leaves others with more work to do)

- Competition between groups or departments for limited resources (including office space, finance, information, status and power). This is a major cause of conflict, whether we're talking about individuals or nations!

- Unfair treatment (eg a manager gives an unfairly harsh evaluation, or refuses legitimate requests for help)

- Hurtful treatment (eg a team member is bullying, offensive, sexist or racist).

Differences, frustrations and competition by themselves don't necessarily lead to conflict: they can even be positive forces, helping people to solve problems or to lift their performance. However, they can escalate or deteriorate into harmful conflict if there is a lack of communication and problem-solving – or if work demands put pressure on people and situations.

Disagreement

It is important that you are able to disagree with someone – and still maintain good working relations! For example, suppose that your supervisor believes that one method of dealing with purchase invoices is the most efficient, but you have a different view. If you have tried to persuade your supervisor that your method is more efficient, but have failed to do so, you need to accept the superior authority, forget the argument and continue with your tasks. It is more important to be effective than to be right!

More serious conflicts

Other disagreements or conflicts may be more serious: someone may be disobeying agreed rules or procedures, say, or behaving in unacceptable or even illegal ways (eg in the case of sexual harassment, bullying or breaking safety rules).

You need to be aware of the limits of your authority to deal with such problems. You may be able to sort some out yourself (eg by having an honest talk with a colleague about how his or her behaviour affects you or the team). In some instances, however, you may need to take it to a higher authority: a process called 'ESCALATION'. We will consider a range of conflict resolution options below.

Effects of unresolved conflict and dissatisfaction

If conflict and dissatisfaction are allowed to go unresolved, or to get worse, they can have a negative impact on the functioning and effectiveness of the team.

- Individuals with unresolved dissatisfactions may become resentful, de-motivated and unco-operative. They may withdraw their contribution to the group – or actively seek to sabotage it.

- The cause of the dissatisfaction may itself be a barrier to effective performance (eg lack of resources).

- Unresolved conflict between individuals can result in reduced communication, co-ordination and co-operation between them.

- Conflict between individuals may split the team into 'factions', escalating rivalry and hostility within the team

- Conflict can polarise differing viewpoints, causing people to hold extreme views, and to dig their heals in, in disagreements. This may make it impossible to 'agree to disagree' – and create unbalanced and risky decisions.

In other words, unresolved conflict can significantly interfere with team working! On the other hand, the effective management of conflict and dissatisfaction can contribute to better team work – and to more productive working relationships.

Law and policy frameworks for positive working relations

Major legislation in the UK and EU is directed at preventing harassment and discrimination against people at work due to their sex or sexual orientation, race or ethnicity, religion, age or disability. This is broadly called 'equal opportunity' law.

Employers must not discriminate in giving people access to jobs, promotion, training or benefits, and you may have rights as a job applicant or employee in these areas. However, employees are also required not to 'harass' others in the workplace by using language or behaviour which intimidates, denigrates or offends.

It is said that 'the law is a floor': it only sets minimum standards of acceptable behaviour. Organisational policies and practices (together with professional codes of conduct) may go beyond basic non-discrimination, to try and foster positive values for working relationships, such as: courtesy, respect, professionalism and team work.

RESOLVING CONFLICTS AND DISSATISFACTIONS

Dealing with dissatisfactions

Some dissatisfactions at work may be within your competence and authority to resolve yourself, or by informal negotiation with your supervisor or colleagues. If your workload is too heavy, for example, you may be able to adjust your schedule or work plans, or ask a colleague to help you. If you get headaches from inadequate light at your desk, you may be able to re-position your desk, or requisition a desk lamp, or ask colleagues' permission to keep window blinds open.

Some dissatisfactions, however, may be *beyond* your competence or authority to resolve yourself. In such cases, you may need to take the problem first to your immediate supervisor or line manager, who may be able to propose or mobilise solutions to the problem.

You may be advised to refer the problem to another appropriate person. If your dissatisfaction is with poor training, for example, you may be advised to approach the Training or HR manager. If you are frustrated by the performance of the office cleaners, you might be advised to communicate with the office manager.

Conflicts you can resolve yourself

Conflicts can be managed informally in several ways.

- If you have a problem working with someone, you might initially attempt direct, informal discussion with the person concerned. Where there is a personality or style clash, this gets the problem out in the open and gives an opportunity to clear up any misunderstandings.

- Problems of incompatible working styles or excessive work demands are matters which can be taken to your supervisor, who will be able to help you develop solutions to the problem.

- If your conflict is with someone in authority over you, you may have to discuss the matter with someone higher up in the organisation. This is probably best handled using more formal channels, called 'grievance procedures' – discussed later.

Where the interests or styles of different parties are genuinely incompatible, you may need to work together to explore a range of options that will at least partially satisfy both parties. This is a process called NEGOTIATION. You may have to give or concede something the other party wants in return for getting something that *you* want: a process of bargaining, which often results in a mutually acceptable compromise.

However, the best approach – most satisfying for both parties *and* most likely to preserve positive relationships – is to attempt to find a mutually satisfying or 'win win' solution. The 'win win' model states that there are three basic ways in which a conflict or problem can be worked out:

- One party gets what (s)he wants at the expense of the other: 'win lose'. For example, if two parties are fighting over an orange, one gets the orange, and the other gets nothing. However well-justified the solution, there is often lingering resentment on the part of the 'losing' party.

- A compromise solution is found, so that neither party gets what (s)he really wanted: 'lose lose'. For example: both parties get half an orange each. However 'logical' such a solution is, there is often lingering dissatisfaction on both sides.

- Both parties work together to understand each other's needs and concerns, and generate options to try and get as close as possible to what each party really wants: 'win win'. A 'win win' result may not be possible, but in the *process* of working together and trying to get the best outcome for both sides, new options may be created – and co-operation will be enhanced. So for example, it may come out in discussion that one party likes orange juice, while another wants the zest of the orange to make a cake: there is now a way of dividing up the orange that leaves *both* parties satisfied!

Task 5

Two of your team members are arguing over who gets to use the desk by the window. Suggest three solutions to this situation, on the basis of

(i)   win-lose
(ii)   compromise
(iii)   win-win

What result can you foresee from each solution?

If personality clash is the main source of conflict, you may have to arrange (or request) a way of working with the other person as little as possible. If the problems persist, you may need to refer them upwards: to have your supervisor (or another appropriate third party) mediate – or arrange for you to work in different areas or teams.

Referring conflicts upwards

In many cases, conflicts and dissatisfactions can be dealt with by the individuals involved. In other cases, however, they may be beyond your authority or ability to resolve, and may require escalation.

It may be necessary to report the incident or conflict to a more senior person for help in handling it. Your supervisor or manager may be able to make decisions to resolve the matter (eg by reallocating resources or changing schedules), or may be in a position to enforce rules and procedures – or may simply be more persuasive getting a point across than you are!

In the first instance, you should go to your supervisor – or whoever has authority over both parties in the conflict. For a conflict within a project team, for example, you might talk to the team leader.

If your conflict is with your own supervisor or line manager, the problem may have to be escalated 'up the line' to his or her immediate manager. Obviously, you will have to think carefully about whether and how you do this. Is the issue serious enough to risk damaging your working relationship with your boss? Do you have a strong, reasonable 'case', supported by evidence, for any allegations you feel you need to make? Can the issue be put in a positive light, with the aim of co-operative problem-solving, in the interests of improving working relationships and work performance?

HOW IT WORKS

Back at Southfield Electronics, Ron did not take well your courteous refusal to take on extra work at short notice. He shouted at you and stormed out of the office. The following day, when he came in late, he was rude to you, and blamed you loudly for his being behind on his work. He says that your 'unco-operative behaviour' will be reflected on your performance appraisal.

What should you do?

You calmly but assertively explain to Ron that you did in fact attempt to be as helpful as possible, but that you had prior work commitments that could not be broken. You refer him, once again, to Kellie McDonald, so that they can resolve the 'time-sharing' issue between them.

If Ron continues to be aggressive and hostile in his manner towards you, you will seek a confidential meeting with Jenny Faulkner (the financial accountant) to explain the situation to her.

Jenny may be able to meet with Kellie and Ron (to resolve the issue of how your time is allocated) and perhaps with you and Ron (to resolve the conflict between you). She will be able to discipline Ron, if necessary, for his inappropriate behaviour.

Formal grievance procedures

In some cases, the matter may be so serious that a more formal approach needs to be adopted.

A GRIEVANCE is a formal complaint by an individual who feels that (s)he is being wrongly or unfairly treated by a colleague or manager at work. Such complaints may include:

- Harassment or bullying

- Unfair or discriminatory treatment by managers due to race, gender or disability

- An employee being given an unfair workload

- An employee being unfairly blocked for promotion.

All organisations should have a written GRIEVANCE PROCEDURE which is communicated to all employees. This should state to whom an employee should go with a particular type of grievance. It will often be his or her line manager. If the grievance is against the line manager, or if it cannot be sorted out at that level, a more senior manager will be consulted, and the HR department may become involved.

If the grievance cannot be sorted out internally, the employee may have to take the problem before an Employment Tribunal, which works as an independent informal court.

CHAPTER OVERVIEW

- Team working, as opposed to working individually, can provide additional resources, inspiration, motivation and communication (for co-ordination).

- When a team is set up, it is important to establish a mix and balance of members; shared, appropriate resources; and agreed working methods, time scales and schedules.

- It may be necessary to provide assistance or support to other team members from time to time, in order to achieve the objectives of the team.

- There will often be conflicts in working relationships, which may be caused by differences in personality, working style or status, or work demands.

- In general, disagreements or conflicts should be dealt with in such a way as to maintain relations and relationships. This requires positive, assertive communication.

- In some cases, conflicts can be satisfactorily dealt with between individuals, but in more serious cases an employee may have to report a matter to a line manager with the authority to resolve matters or enforce rules.

- Employers should have a written grievance procedure policy which employees can follow if the grievance needs to be properly investigated and arbitrated by senior management.

Keywords

Team – a group of employees working together to meet shared objectives

Co-ordination – the process by which the work of different individuals and teams is linked together to achieve shared objectives

Synergy – a process in team working by which 'the whole is greater than the sum of its parts' – or $2 + 2 = 5$

Virtual team – a team linked wholly or mainly by ICT tools such as the internet

Assertive communication – a style of communication based on respecting your own rights – without trampling on the rights of others

Conflict – opposing forces or interests, causing disagreement, competition or hostility

Escalation – taking a problem to a higher level of management for resolution

Negotiation – a process of bargaining to reach a solution in a situation where there is a conflict of interests

Grievance – a complaint brought by an employee who feels wrongly treated by colleagues or managers

Grievance procedure – an employer's formalised procedure for investigating and resolving a grievance

TEST YOUR LEARNING

Test 1

Give three examples of teams that might operate within an accounting function.

Test 2

Explain the main advantages of working in a team rather than individually.

Test 3

Give examples of roles that people might occupy in a well-balanced team.

Test 4

If a team is working to complete a particular project, why is it important that all schedules and timetables are (a) agreed and (b) met?

Test 5

Explain how mutual assistance within a team can provide synergies.

Test 6

You have recently joined the accounting department of a company and have found one of your fellow accounts assistants to be extremely rude to you and constantly demanding that you fetch the coffee, clean up the kitchen etc.

What action could you take to deal with this?

Test 7

If you disagree with a decision being made, and wish to influence the decision maker, what style of communication should you use to communicate with him or her?

Test 8

You and a colleague both need access to the same file at the same time. You both need it to compile reports for your managers, for the following morning. It is now 3.00pm and each of you will need it for two hours to do this work. Suggest (a) a win-lose, (b) compromise and (c) a win-win solution in the scenario. What result can you foresee from each solution?

Test 9

You are reading *Student Accountant* magazine, and encounter a letter to the editor ('Don't wipe your feet on the doormat', 23/04/X0) complaining about a bullying colleague. The writer says that she cannot stand up to this person, because she does not wish to be seen as 'selfish' or 'aggressive' in the work place. Write a letter to the editor (at the editorial office: 3 Graves St, Bristol, BR3 3NG) setting out what you take to be the basis of assertive communication.

Test 10

Since you started work in the accounts department, you have had some personal conflicts with one of the other accounts assistants, George Moss. Since day one, he has constantly picked on you as the most recent recruit, forcing you to make his coffee and do his photocopying for him. However, recently things have got worse and you now find that when George cannot finish his own tasks on time (which happens fairly frequently), he asks you to help him complete them. To date, you have been happy to help, as you find that you often manage to finish your own tasks within the working day. However, you are now beginning to realise that George is handing over tasks to you so that he can spend more time chatting to colleagues and on the telephone. You do not want to seem unco-operative, but you do feel that you are being used by a less than conscientious colleague.

How would you deal with this situation?

Test 11

Give examples of possible 'grievances' in the workplace.

chapter 8:
DEVELOPING SKILLS AND KNOWLEDGE

chapter coverage 📖

This chapter considers how each individual can develop the skills and knowledge required to meet both their own and the organisation's needs.

It explains how to identify your own development needs and to formulate your own personal development plan: a task that you may be required to carry out in your assessment. It also contains information regarding the importance of continuing professional development and on monitoring your own development progress, which you may need to refer to when carrying out the tasks in your assessment.

The topics covered are:

- ✍ Continuing professional development
- ✍ Identifying your development needs
- ✍ Defining your development objectives
- ✍ Learning and development approaches
- ✍ Monitoring and reviewing your progress
- ✍ Your personal development plan

CONTINUING PROFESSIONAL DEVELOPMENT

Let's start with some useful definitions.

- TRAINING is a process of using learning experiences to achieve more effective performance in particular work activities or roles.

- DEVELOPMENT is a broader process of growth in knowledge and capabilities. In addition to education and training, individuals may be encouraged to gain experience of different roles in an organisation, and increasing challenges (perhaps through promotion within the organisation, or 'career development').

- CONTINUING PROFESSIONAL DEVELOPMENT (CPD) is a systematic process of planning for the future and of gaining experience and training relevant to the directions in which they want to develop – both within the current job role, and in future career progression.

Members of professional bodies (such as the AAT, CIMA or ICAEW) are required to complete a certain amount of CPD as a condition of continuing membership. This ensures that their knowledge and skills are always up-to-date and of a good standard. This, in turn, protects the interests of their clients and employers, as well as the standing and credibility of the professional bodies and the accounting profession.

As we will see, Continuing Professional Development (CPD) can be pursued in a number of different ways. Individuals may undertake vocational training through the NVQ framework, or further education through universities and colleges. They may study for progression to membership of a professional body (like the AAT). They may receive instruction, training or coaching in the workplace. Or they may plan for self-development by a continual process of identifying their weaknesses, seeking opportunities to practice, gathering feedback, and learning from their mistakes.

A key feature of the CPD approach is that the responsibility for development lies mainly with the individual, in collaboration with his or her employers, and other parties such as the professional bodies.

You are responsible for maintaining CPD appropriate to:

- *Your current job role*: helping you to meet the requirements of the role better – and ensuring that you stay up-to-date with the changing requirements of the role, and/or changing developments in your field

- *Your career aspirations:* equipping yourself with the knowledge and skills you will require for higher-level roles, and enabling you to seek more challenging job opportunities.

Why is training and development important?

Training can represent a significant cost to a business – in terms of training costs (training providers and resources), staff time spent in training, and resulting lost production – or the costs of covering training absences with replacement staff or overtime working.

It is, therefore, important to be able to *justify* training effort and expenditure on the basis of sound business benefits!

The on-going development of skills and knowledge has significant benefits for the learners/trainees themselves, and for the organisation in which they work.

Benefits for the individual	Benefits for the employing organisation
Greater confidence and flexibility	More competent job performance
Improved job performance (perhaps leading to increased rewards and recognition)	Competent performance achieved more quickly by new recruits
Greater job security	Less supervision required
Ability to take on more challenge and responsibility in the job	Increased efficiency and productivity, through faster, more skilled work
Increased prospects of promotion	Reduced cost of errors, reduced non-compliance with regulations/laws
Enhanced skills, which can be used outside the job (eg communication skills)	Supports employee initiative, ideas, flexibility and innovation
Satisfaction from greater contribution	Improved staff motivation and morale
Greater 'employability' and value in the job market	Enhanced ability to recruit and retain high-quality employees

Task 1

You have recently prepared, and agreed with your supervisor (Mrs Hoff), a Personal Development Plan, showing targets and activities for your learning over the next six months. Having submitted this plan to the HR Manager (Mr Bolt), you receive the following email.

EMAIL

From: a.bolt@reeves.co.uk
To: y.name@reeves.co.uk; g.hoff@reeves.co.uk
Date: [Today's date]
Re: Personal Development Plan

Thank you for submitting Your Name's PDP for the next six months.

I am somewhat concerned at the cost of such plans for the Accounts department as a whole. Every member of the department has submitted requests for training – and also for 'professional development' activity which does not seem to be directly related to their current job roles.

I am not sure that this can be justified, and will have to review the PDPs and training requests in this light.

Mrs Hoff asks you to email Mr Bolt in reply, explaining the importance and benefits of Continuing Professional Development.

IDENTIFYING YOUR DEVELOPMENT NEEDS

Learning needs and career goals are highly specific to each individual – and to particular work contexts and roles. Obviously, we can't tell you what your career aspirations are (or should be), what your strengths and weaknesses are, or what areas of knowledge or skill you may need to develop further. What we *can* do is to give you the tools to work these things out for yourself – whether in your workplace, or in your assessment.

Identifying learning needs in your current job

The most obvious starting point for identifying learning needs may be: how well do I fulfil the requirements of my current work role?

To answer this question, you can simply think through what it is that you do on a day-to-day basis, or consider feedback you have received from your supervisor or line manager about your performance. You may receive more formal feedback reports, setting out recommendations for learning and development, from performance reviews or appraisals.

For a systematic 'start-from-scratch' analysis, you might start with two key documents used by organisations to define the requirements of a job and of a job-holder.

- Your JOB DESCRIPTION or role description, which sets out what a person in your job should be able to do. It describes the requirements of the job.

- The PERSON SPECIFICATION for your role, which sets out what sort of personal qualities the organisation is looking for in your role. It describes the requirements of the job-holder.

Having got to grips with what is required of you in your job, you can ask yourself some questions. Do I have the knowledge and skills necessary to perform my tasks competently? What tasks in my job description am I not yet able to perform well? What desirable attributes in the person specification for my role do I currently lack? Putting this all together: what are my strengths and weaknesses in this role?

HOW IT WORKS

When you joined Southfield Electronics, you were shown the following documents relating to your job role.

JOB DESCRIPTION	
Job title:	Accounts clerk, financial accounting
Location:	London office
Job summary:	General financial accounting duties
Key responsibilities	Administrative support for the financial accounts section, including opening post and handling telephone and email enquiries
	Obtaining quotes from suppliers
	Preparing daily cheque listings, sales invoices, credit notes and monthly sales summaries (using computer spreadsheets)
	Monthly sales ledger control account reconciliation
	Responsibility for petty cash in the cashier's absence
Reporting structure:	Financial accountant
	|
	Assistant financial accountants (2) and Payroll manager
	|
	Accounts clerk
Hours:	9.00 am to 5.30 pm Monday to Friday 1 hour for lunch
Training:	Induction training will be provided Continuing Professional Development encouraged
Prepared by:	Head of HR
Date:	March 20X0

PERSON SPECIFICATION		
CRITERIA	**ESSENTIAL**	**DESIRABLE**
Qualifications	GCSE English Language (Grade A* – C)	Undertaking AAT Level 2 qualification
	GCSE Mathematics (Grade A* – C)	Level 2 Word processing
		Level 2 Spreadsheets
Experience	Basic computer use	Previous accounts or clerical/administrative experience
	General office procedures	

PERSON SPECIFICATION		
CRITERIA	ESSENTIAL	DESIRABLE
Communication	Ability to communicate effectively in a range of situations Understanding of the importance of confidentiality	Familiarity with different communication formats
Team working	Ability to work flexibly in a team Understanding of deadlines	Previous experience of working in a team
Personal skills/ attributes	Personal integrity Attention to detail Ability to handle pressure	Ability to work without supervision when required

You now want to put together some ideas about your training needs, for your up-coming review. You decide to start with your current job performance. Is there room for improvement in the way you fulfil the requirements set out in the job description and person specification?

You make the following notes in your Personal Development Journal.

- *Do I have the knowledge and skills necessary to perform my tasks competently?*

  I still struggle with the monthly ledger control account reconciliation, which I know takes me longer than it should. This is not helped by the fact that I am not confident about double entry bookkeeping. Whenever I have to prepare a computer spreadsheet, I have to ask one of the other accounts assistants for help, as I don't know how to do it on my own.

- *What tasks in my job description am I not yet able to perform well?*

  I should be responsible for petty cash when the cashier is absent, but I have never been asked to do this nor do I know how to.

- *What desirable attributes in the person specification for my role do I currently lack?*

  The holder of my role should ideally have a Level 2 qualification in Spreadsheets, and I have not yet attained this.

From these answers, you are able to draw up a list of your most immediate learning needs.

Learning needs to improve in my current job

- I would benefit from help from a senior colleague to show me how to perform the sales ledger (receivables ledger) reconciliation more efficiently.

- I would benefit from studying a textbook on double entry bookkeeping – or perhaps a short bookkeeping course

---

> - I should plan to attend a computer spreadsheet course or get instruction from a colleague, with a view to working towards a Level 2 qualification.
>
> - I should ask to spend some time with the cashier being shown how she deals with petty cash claims, and, perhaps, perform the task a few times under her supervision.

Strengths and weaknesses analysis

A more general approach to identifying your learning needs would be to review the requirements of your role and your performance in the role, and then to ask, simply: what are my strengths and weaknesses in this role?

- Identified *strengths* are areas that you can build on. They may represent a foundation for further learning – or areas in which you are ready to ask for more challenge or responsibility.

- Identified *weaknesses* are areas that need attention in order to bring your competence or confidence up to the required level. They may represent your most immediate learning needs.

HOW IT WORKS

Continuing your learning needs planning at Southfield Electronics, you review your job description and person specification, and note the various requirements of your current role. How well are you fulfilling those requirements?

You reflect on your *own performance*, remembering particular incidents that have highlighted good and bad points: finishing your workload early so that you could help other members of the project team; mistakes you made in your double entry book-keeping; having to ask for help with the computer spreadsheets, because you didn't feel confident about doing them on your own...

You note down the *feedback* you have received from others on your performance: your supervisor's praise for well-written reports and emails; a colleague's comment that the sales ledger reconciliation is taking you longer than it should...

You look at the tasks in the *job description* that you are (and are not yet) performing well, and the attributes in the *person specification* that you do (and do not yet) possess.

You now have a list of good points and bad points, and you decide to pick the three most important of each to build or work on.

STRENGTHS	WEAKNESSES
1. Efficient workload management, prioritisation and flexibility to help others	1. Lack of full competence in double entry bookkeeping and sales ledger reconciliation
2. Effective communication using emails and reports	2. Lack of confidence in preparing computer spreadsheets: not yet attained Level 2 qualification
3. Good ability to work without supervision and under pressure when required	3. Lack of knowledge/experience of petty cash procedures

Now you can draw up a list of learning objectives which will:

(a) Build on your strengths: you will volunteer to act as secretary to your next project team, in order to develop your communication and workload management skills further

(b) Address your identified weaknesses: you will plan learning activities to improve your double entry bookkeeping, sales ledger reconciliation, use of computer spreadsheets, and knowledge of petty cash procedures.

Task 2

You are the account's clerk at Southfield Electronics. The requirements of your job role are defined by the job description and person specification provided in the 'How It Works' section earlier.

Based on your *own real life* knowledge, skills, experience and attributes, carry out a strengths and weaknesses analysis, and suggest how you will go about building on your strengths and addressing your weaknesses.

Other tools for learning needs analysis

Some organisations carry out formal learning needs analysis, by *testing* employees' performance on areas listed in a job description or competence definition, say, or by discussing learning needs as part of their annual *performance appraisals*.

Other approaches include:

- Keeping a Personal Development Journal, in which you note down any incidents at work which indicate a learning need (eg having to ask for assistance, making a mistake or getting a complaint or negative feedback from a colleague). These are sometimes called 'critical incidents', as they highlight an underlying issue or need.

- Scanning the office notice board, intranet pages or staff magazines for advertised training courses and opportunities which strike you as relevant to your job.

- Gathering feedback or assessments from each training course you undertake, pointing you to 'areas for further improvement' or follow-up learning.

- Asking your supervisor or colleagues for feedback on areas of your performance: 'What do you think I need to learn about or do better?' (An excellent source of information, particularly about your interpersonal skills, or how you work with others!)

Identifying learning needs to fit your future career aspirations

Although you may be happy with your current job role, most people do have ambitions to develop their career, for personal satisfaction and growth – and for higher status and rewards. In order to identify future learning needs, you will need to consider where you are aiming for – whether within your current organisation or elsewhere. What are your CAREER GOALS?

Ambition is a helpful motivator for personal development – but take care to be *realistic* in your goals. As a first year accounts assistant, it may be realistic to aspire to become an accounts supervisor, but perhaps *not* to aspire to be Finance Director within two years! Factor in any learning, experience, maturing and trust-earning that may be required to get from where you are to where you want to get to…

It may help to talk informally to colleagues and those in more senior roles about how they got to their positions. It may also be useful to have a more formal conversation with your line manager or the Human Resources manager, to determine the realistic career goals for you as an individual – and what support and opportunities may be available within the organisation.

Once you have identified some goals, you need to plan how to get from your current position to the job that you aspire to.

First, you need to ensure that you are carrying out your current role efficiently and effectively! Then you must consider the requirements of the job that you wish to have.

You may need to talk to your line manager or Human Resources manager in order to find out the details of the knowledge, skills and any qualifications that are required for this job. Once you are armed with this information, you can begin to set yourself realistic and specific development objectives – just as you would for your current job role.

DEFINING YOUR DEVELOPMENT OBJECTIVES

Even if your organisation supports you in training and development planning, it is important that you define your own development objectives, within the context of your own strengths, weaknesses and career goals.

Effective objectives (whether for knowledge and skills development or for career development) are SMART:

S	Specific
M	Measurable
A	Agreed
R	Realistic
T	Time-bounded

Specific

Specificity is necessary in order for a plan of action to be drawn up. 'To improve my use of spreadsheets soon' is far too vague to suggest an action plan – or to get you motivated! 'To pass the AAT Level 2 Spreadsheet assessment by October' is a much better guide to what (exactly) you want to do!

Try to be exact about what you hope to achieve or be able to do.

Measurable

You need to be able to review how you are progressing towards your goals – and whether you've reached them – so you need to state your objectives in a way that will enable you to measure or assess your performance.

How will you (or others) know how much progress you've made? How will you (or others) define completion or success? What test will you be able to pass? What will you be able to do that you couldn't do before? (Note that your Learning Outcomes for this Unit are designed to be measurable in this way.)

Plan up front for when, how often and how your progress towards meeting the objective will be monitored and reviewed.

Agreed

In many cases the achievement of development objectives will require the commitment of resources from your employer: the loss of your time while you study or train, the costs of training, your manager's time coaching you and so on. Therefore, it is important that any personal development objectives are agreed with your supervisor or line manager. (Some matters may be referred to the Training manager or Human Resources manager for further planning and negotiation of goals and resources.)

Realistic

You need to ensure that your objectives are achievable, taking into account the various constraints under which you operate – time, resources, ability and current commitments. Break the objectives down into smaller, manageable chunks, if necessary.

Time-bounded

Include a time scale within which the objective is to be achieved. 'To complete Level 2 Spreadsheets' is the start of an objective but is this within a two-year time scale or a ten-year time scale? 'To complete Level 2 Spreadsheets within six months (or by a particular date)' is a much better development objective. Make sure your time scale is realistic, too!

LEARNING AND DEVELOPMENT APPROACHES

Your learning objectives will in most cases involve acquiring new skills and knowledge for current and future job challenges. So how will you go about this? It will require research into specific opportunities relevant to your SMART objectives, but some of the sources of CPD you may consider are as follows.

Technical briefings and updates

If you want to enhance your knowledge on a topic relevant to your work, or to keep your knowledge up-to-date, you might seek out technical briefings and updates. These may be provided by technical experts within your organisation, or by external bodies. HM Revenue and Customs, for example, may offer update seminars on topics such as VAT, payroll, income/corporate tax, and online reporting. Professional bodies (such as AAT, CIMA and ICAEW) similarly offer technical seminars and local branch events on topics relevant to their field.

You should also look out for technical briefings and updates provided by such bodies in printed form (mailed or emailed to subscribers), or posted on their web sites. Your organisation may keep a library of such resources.

Training courses and seminars

One of the most obvious ways of enhancing your skills and knowledge is by attending training courses and seminars. These may be run internally by your organisation or by external training providers. (External courses can be researched by contacting a local college of further education or by using the internet.) They may be short, stand-alone knowledge- or skills- based courses (eg a course in effective communication, team lead or using spreadsheets), or they may be part of a longer scheme of study towards an academic, vocational or professional qualification.

The key advantage of training courses is that they generally give you access to experts, in a structured environment which is designed to maximise learning. There is a disadvantage to 'off-the-job' learning, however, in that it may not be easy to transfer or apply what you have learned in the workplace.

The internet

The internet can be used to find details of local course providers and CPD events. It may also be a source of information relevant to your learning needs. For example, you could use a search engine such as Google to find articles on assertiveness or managing conflict in the workplace; websites offering technical and legal updates; or tips and tools for various accounting tasks. There may also be web-based courses (or e-learning) in your areas of interest.

Publications

Most industries and professions have specialist journals or trade publications, which may include articles relevant to your learning needs. It may be worth subscribing to a publication of this kind, in order to keep up-to-date with developments in your profession and business sector. Your organisation or department may have a library of relevant journals that you could use, or you may be able to browse the online versions.

Books are another useful learning tool. If you have doubts about your double entry bookkeeping skills, for example, one option is to invest in a textbook and work through it in your own time.

Other research tools

In addition to information searches in publications and the internet, you might consider research tools such as: arranging to talk to (or get instruction from) experts in a topic or skill; or visiting work sites and other places where relevant procedures and practices are demonstrated.

You might also seek out opportunities to try out skills or procedures yourself (where it is not too great a risk to yourself or others to do so!), and then gather feedback on your performance and what you need to do better or differently next time: this is called 'experiential learning' or learning by doing. It is an important tool for on-the-job learning.

Colleagues and coaches

One of the most neglected sources of information and learning is work colleagues. They may be able to give you advice on training courses to attend or books or journals to read. You may also be able to learn new skills from colleagues, through instruction or coaching. Don't forget the 'phone a friend' option!

You may find that you can also simply watch more experienced colleagues at work, to learn from their methods, procedures, techniques and behaviour. This observation may take place informally as you work with colleagues, or on a more formal 'shadowing' or coaching basis.

Task 3

Suggest a suitable learning or training approach for each of the following learning needs.

(a)   A worker is transferred onto a new piece of equipment and needs to learn how to operate it.

(b)   An accounts clerk wishes to work toward becoming AAT qualified.

(c)   An organisation decides that its supervisors would benefit from ideas on team leadership.

(d)   A new member of staff is about to join the organisation.

MONITORING AND REVIEWING YOUR PROGRESS

There is no point in setting an objective if you are not prepared to review your progress and achievements on a regular basis. Regular monitoring and review is important in:

- Allowing you to measure your progress towards your goal, so that you are motivated to 'keep on track'

- Allowing you to identify any mistakes or weaknesses in your current performance, so that you can use them in your learning

- Identifying where you are 'off track' or 'behind schedule' on your development plan, so that you can adjust your effort and activity as required

- Identifying where your goals or plans were unrealistic and need adjustment

- Keeping you accountable to your supervisor, coach or line manager for agreed learning goals and progress

- Enabling your supervisor or line manager to justify the costs of your training and development, in terms of proven results and benefits

- Ensuring that the costs of training and development are not being wasted or used inefficiently

- Ensuring that measurable business benefits are accruing to the organisation from your development

- Enabling you to celebrate improvements and attainments (an important part of staying motivated – and reaping the benefits of development).

Informally monitoring progress

You can monitor your own progress against your goals on a regular basis. For example, have you kept up-to-date in your reading on technical changes that affect your job? Have you booked yourself on to the training course that you decided would be a necessary part of your personal development? Are you having to ask for help less frequently? Have you attained the targets you set?

Another review method is to get informal feedback from your supervisor or colleagues. Have they noticed a change in your performance or behaviour? Do they think you have met the targets you set for yourself? How do they think you have improved – and could improve still further?

Formal evaluation and review

In many cases, there will be more formal methods of evaluation and review. Most organisations plan periodic progress reviews (especially in project work and for new recruits). There will also probably be annual PERFORMANCE APPRAISAL for all employees.

You can also use a Personal Development Plan (discussed in a moment) to:

- Set specific criteria for measurement of your progress and attainment

- Gain the co-operation of your supervisor or coach in reviewing your progress at defined intervals or times, and giving you helpful feedback on your progress and performance

- Gain the co-operation of your supervisor in arranging formal testing of your progress or attainment (eg competence assessment, or on-the-job observation).

Such mechanisms allow you systematically to measure your progress against agreed goals, get feedback from your supervisor (and other relevant parties), review your learning objectives, and identify and agree further learning needs.

YOUR PERSONAL DEVELOPMENT PLAN

Having come this far, you have all the tools necessary to formulate a more formal and systematic PERSONAL DEVELOPMENT PLAN or PDP.

A PDP is a clear developmental action plan, which once agreed with the individual's supervisor or line manager, acts as a 'learning contract' between them.

You may have your own preferences for formatting and recording action plans: timetables, diaries, checklists and other methods covered in Chapter 6, for example. Be sure to use any format recommended by your work organisation – or suggested by the assessment case study.

In the absence of such guidelines, feel free to use whatever works for you – but we recommend a simple, systematic format such as the following.

Objective	Methods	Timescale	Monitoring/review
Concise statement of your SMART learning objective	Specific learning methods and activities selected	Target completion date for each listed learning method or activity	How, with whom and how often you will check your progress

HOW IT WORKS

Back at Southfield Electronics, having identified some immediate learning needs to improve your job performance, you prepare the following Personal Development Plan for the next six months, which you agree with Kellie McDonald (your designated Learning Supervisor).

Objective	Method	Timescale	Monitoring/review
To be able to perform petty cash operations	Coaching: instruction and supervised practice with the cashier	By last week of September	Practice tasks under the cashier's supervision and seek feedback
To be able to perform double entry book-keeping tasks with 100% accuracy, without assistance	Reading: review Basic Accounting Textbook Training: short external bookkeeping course	By last week of October Completed by last week of October	Practice tasks, checked by Kellie McDonald End of course competency test
To be able to perform sales ledger reconciliations efficiently, without assistance	Reading: review Basic Accounting Textbook Coaching: ask Kellie McDonald to instruct and coach me on the process	First week of November By third week of November	Review progress with Kellie during coaching Practice at end October, and seek feedback from Kellie
To achieve the Level 2 Spreadsheets qualification	Training: short computer spreadsheet course	Completed by end of February	End of course competency test Feedback from Ron Howard on application at work

Including your supervisor or line manager in the planning process

Personal Development Planning puts the onus on the individual to define development goals which are relevant to them, and to seek out learning opportunities which suit their needs, preferences and opportunities.

However, it is vitally important to include your supervisor, line manager or designated coach in the process, so that (s)he can:

- Check that your goals are SMART, and of potential benefit to the department and organisation

- Check that the learning activities selected are suitable and cost-effective for the organisation

- Suggest learning methods and opportunities that you might not be aware of

- Mobilise learning opportunities and resources (eg by recommending you for a training course, providing access to publications, or appointing a coach or mentor)

- Authorise and arrange the time off and expenditure that will be required for your training (including cover for your absences, where relevant)

- Plan to participate, as required, in your learning (eg by acting as a coach or providing feedback) and in monitoring and review of your progress.

Recording your CPD activity

As we noted at the beginning of this chapter, members of professional bodies are required to complete a certain number of hours of CPD, in order to ensure that they maintain their technical competence and up-to-date knowledge. You must therefore record any CPD activity you undertake, so that you can prove that you have fulfilled the requirements and updated your knowledge and skills appropriately.

Online tools for recording CPD activity are available to AAT members via the AAT web site.

HOW IT WORKS

Southfield Electronics encourages all accounts staff to maintain a CPD log, which is reviewed alongside each individual's Personal Development Plan. The company uses a simple pro forma log sheet for CPD activity.

CONTINUING PROFESSIONAL DEVELOPMENT RECORD

Name:... Membership no: ....

Covering the period from: .... to ....

Date(s)	CPD hours	Links to PDP goal	Learning activity	Training provider	Outcomes/ benefits	Follow-up required

Continuing professional development: a *continuous* process!

Just to finish this chapter it should be noted that the setting of personal development objectives, their review, appraisal and updating will be a continuous process throughout your working career – not simply a one-off exercise!

CHAPTER OVERVIEW

- You need to maintain and update your knowledge and skills to keep pace with technical, legal, technological and other developments affecting your profession and job role. This is called Continuing Professional Development, and it is compulsory for members of professional bodies, as a condition of membership.

- It is important to be able to justify the costs and time devoted to training and development activity. Learning benefits the individual and their employing organisation in a wide variety of ways.

- When considering your own development needs, the best starting point is the current job that you perform. What additional skills or knowledge do you require to carry out your role more effectively and efficiently? What strengths and weaknesses can you identify in the way you fulfil the requirements of your job, as defined by your job description and/or person specification?

- Most employees will have ambitions for career development. Consider your own career goals and what additional skills and knowledge will be required in order for you to achieve them. Remember to be realistic.

- Begin to set your own personal development objectives. Check that they are SMART – specific, measurable, agreed, realistic and time-bounded.

- Sources of CPD activity include: technical updates, training courses and seminars, the internet, journals and trade publications, books, colleagues and observation of others.

- Once personal development objectives have been set, progress must be monitored, reviewed and evaluated. This may be a process of self-review, feedback from others or formal appraisal.

- Be prepared to formulate a Personal Development Plan for your own role, and for any role you are assigned in the assessment case study, based on your own identified career goals, competences, strengths and weaknesses.

Keywords

Training – a planned process of using learning experiences to achieve more effective performance, in particular, work activities or roles

Development – growth in your knowledge and capabilities, and increasing fulfilment of your potential

Continuing Professional Development – a process of gaining experience and training relevant to the directions in which you want to develop

Job description – a concise statement of the tasks and responsibilities of a particular job

Person specification – a concise statement of the qualities an organisation wants in the holder of a particular job

Career goals – your aims in terms of the job(s) you aspire to in future

SMART – a framework for setting objectives – they should be specific, measurable, agreed, realistic, time-bounded

Personal Development Plan – a learning plan that can be agreed and monitored by your supervisor or learning coach

Performance appraisal – the formal process of regular review of each individual employee's performance, progress and development objectives

TEST YOUR LEARNING

Test 1

Why is CPD important for members of professional bodies, and why does CPD activity have to be recorded?

Test 2

Explain the benefits of learning and development for an individual employee.

Test 3

What two documents are useful in determining the requirements of a particular job role? Describe what these documents typically contain.

Test 4

You have just received the following email.

EMAIL	
From:	jobloggs@stubbs.com
To:	yourname@stubbs.com
Date:	[Today's date]
Re:	Learning needs analysis

We haven't met yet, but my name is Jo, and I'm new in the cost accounts section. I've been asked to come up with some ideas on 'learning needs' for the end of my induction training, and I'm not sure how to go about this. I was told you've done a learning needs analysis quite recently, and I wondered if you could give me some pointers about how to identify learning needs for my job.

Thanks.

Jo

Draft a reply, giving Jo whatever information you think helpful.

Test 5

In the context of setting personal development objectives, what is meant by each element of the SMART framework?

Test 6

Excluding the internet, briefly explain any four methods for acquiring new skills and knowledge for your work.

Test 7

The internet is a good source of technical information, including information on new laws and regulations. However, if the user is not vigilant he or she could end up obtaining misleading or incorrect technical knowledge.

Describe why this problem arises when using the internet as a source for this information and outline the precautions you could take to prevent this from happening.

Test 8

What would be an appropriate learning approach for the following learning needs?

(a) An employee wants to ensure that she is aware of the latest rules under the Data Protection Act.

(b) An accounts clerk wishes to improve in the use of double-entry bookkeeping and computer spreadsheets.

(c) An accounts clerk wishes to improve his participation in team meetings.

Test 9

Explain four different ways of monitoring and reviewing your progress against your development goals.

Test 10

What issues do you think would be discussed in a typical appraisal session with a line manager?

ANSWERS TO CHAPTER TASKS

CHAPTER 2 The role of the financial functions

Task 1

(a) The payroll department *requires* regular information from the HR and other employing departments, about matters such as: employees' National Insurance details; dates of commencing (or ending) employment; agreed wage/salary and overtime rates; standard and overtime hours worked (eg using time sheets or clock cards); and paid holiday arrangements.

(b) The payroll department provides:

- The HR department and employing departments with information about total wage/salary and overtime costs

- The accounts department with payroll statistics for the recording of costs (and, where there is a separate cashier function, for arranging to make wage/salary payments)

- Individual employees with required information about their pay and deductions

- External agencies with statutory returns (eg tax and National Insurance contributions) and statistical information.

Task 2

EMAIL	
To:	hskommett@southfield.co.uk
From:	yname@southfield.co.uk
Date:	*[today's date]*
Subject:	Cash flow and credit control issues

Hailey, I've been asked by the Chief Accountant to bring to your attention the matter of cash flow and credit control, as highlighted by recent cash flow summaries.

I'm sure you know how important it is to maintain positive cash flow, so that the organisation has sufficient day-to-day funds to maintain its operations and pay its debts. Recently, however, Southfield has been paying out money to suppliers faster than it has been collecting money from customers. The Sales department obviously has a key role in this, through its credit control policies.

The Chief Accountant is keen to review the issues with you and the Purchasing Manager. Could you suggest three or four times/dates when you might be free for a meeting?

Thanks.

YN

CHAPTER 3   The organisational framework

Task 1

(a)   You report directly to three people: Kellie McDonald, Ron Howard and Jane Chu

(b)   NI contributions are a payroll matter, so the natural person to consult would be Jane Chu, the payroll manager

(c)   The two assistant financial accountants and the payroll manager are on the same level of authority

(d)   This might cause you difficulties because if they make excessive or conflicting work demands on you, it will be difficult to know whose work to prioritise: they all have an equal 'right' to exercise authority over you

(e)   You would need to look further up the chain of command, which leads directly to the Financial accountant (Jenny Faulkner)

(f)   The formal line of communication would be to contact him or her via the production manager

(g)   The finance function only has 'staff' (that is, expert, advisory or policy-making) authority over Logistics in areas to do with finance (such as credit control).

Task 2

It depends who has asked you to perform the task. If you were asked by the Accounts manager, you would report directly to him or her. If you were asked by the HR or Training manager (with your line manager's permission), you might report directly to them.

Task 3

EVACUATION PROCEDURES: WHAT YOU MUST DO

- **Leave the building** IMMEDIATELY by the designated route as quickly (but calmly) as possible, not lingering to gather personal belongings
- DO NOT use **lifts** in the event of a fire emergency
- Go immediately to the **designated Assembly** Point and ensure that any visitors are directed and assisted
- Pay particular attention to people with **special needs** (eg those in wheelchairs or with impaired sight or hearing)
- **Respond** when your name is called by the Safety Officer who will 'call a roll' of everyone signed in as being in the building
- DO NOT return to the building until **instructed** to do so by a senior official or the Safety Officer.

It is very important to take part in DRILLS, and to comply with the procedure when doing so. Repeated practice will make us better at evacuation – contributing to all our safety. There is no way of knowing if an alarm is for a drill or 'for real': by failing to take part and follow the procedure, you are endangering your life and the lives of others. Let's all be responsible in co-operating with the safety policy.

Task 4

    (a)   This is confidential information and should not be given. You should tell the enquirer courteously that you are not able, under your company's privacy policy, to give out such information.

    (b)   This is personal information, which may impact on the employees' privacy, and should not be given. You should advise your colleague to ask the other employees for their address.

    (c)   This is not private or confidential information, and is intended to enhance office security. You should comply with the request.

Task 5

You will need to know:

    (a)   What documents are required (eg appropriate form, attached receipts)

    (b)   What value of transactions require authorisation, and at what levels

    (c)   Who the authorising managers or designated signatories are

    (e)   Deadlines for receipt and authorisation

    (f)   How transactions should be processed

    (g)   What you should do if the information is incomplete, incorrectly authorised or otherwise contrary to the policy.

Task 6

EMAIL	
To:	allstaff@southfield.co.uk
From:	yname@southfield.co.uk
Date:	[Today's date]
Subject:	Procedure for cheque requisitions

Having recently received incorrectly completed cheque requisition forms, I thought it might be helpful to remind everyone of the correct procedure.

- All cheque requisitions must be completed legibly and in full

- All requisitions must be accompanied by a VAT receipt or invoice as evidence of payment

- For amounts between £100 and £500, requisitions must be authorised by your department manager

- Correctly completed and authorised forms must be with the accounts department by 10 am for a cheque to be prepared on the same day.

It is important to comply with the procedure, to maintain sound financial control. Forms which are incorrectly completed or authorised will have to be returned to the originator – which wastes everybody's time, and ultimately results in a delay in the issuing of your cheque. I am sure we would all wish to avoid this, so please take every care in complying with the procedure.

CHAPTER 4 Communication skills

Task 1

(a) Order by telephone, confirmed in writing later (by order form or letter) – or email order (if both parties have email access)

(b) Notice board (or employee intranet page, if available) or general meeting: depending on the sensitivity of the topic and the need for staff to be able to ask questions

(c) Face-to-face private conversation – but it would be a good idea to confirm the outcome in writing so that records can be maintained

(d) Telephone, email or face-to-face (if close by)

(e) Face-to-face, supported by clear written notes, enabling you to use visual aids (such as diagrams) to help explain. A meeting will also give you the opportunity to check the group's understanding – while the notes will save them having to memorise what you say, and enable them to focus on understanding.

Task 2

You should explain to your colleague that technical correctness is important:

(a) because other people and operations rely on the information

(b) it is the responsibility of the accounting function to provide complete and accurate information

(c) technical errors waste time in returned work and re-work; and

(d) repeated errors reflect badly on the person making them, and on the department as a whole, and may reduce their credibility in the organisation.

Task 3

One great advantage of word-processed documents is that they can be saved and edited easily. They allow you to make corrections and changes which are 'invisible' to the reader. They also enable you to create standard or 'template' documents (such as requests for quotations, or debt collection letters): each time the document is required, the relevant details can be altered or slotted in (or merged from a database, eg in the case of a personalised, standard letter to all staff or customers).

Task 4

Do...	Don't...
Write in full sentences	Use 'text message'-style abbreviations
Use direct (not ambiguous), commonly used (but not clichéd), and factual (less emotional, less 'colourful') language	Use abbreviated forms such as 'There's', 'I'm', 'We've': use the full forms (there is, I am, we have) instead
Remove digressions, rambles and unnecessary words and phrases: keep to the point.	Use colloquial or slang expressions (like 'This sucks': replace with something like 'This is frustrating' or 'This is unsatisfactory'...)
Refer to people by their title and surname, in more formal relationships – or where their expectations about formality are unknown.	Be overly 'familiar' or friendly in tone, or personal in content, unless the other person has expressly invited this.

Task 5

If a training programme costs £2,300 out of a total of £11,500:

$$\frac{2,300}{11,500} \times 100 = \frac{230,000}{1,150,000} = \frac{1}{5} = 20\%$$

In a pie chart, this would be 20% of a 360° circle:

$$\frac{20}{100} \times 360 = \text{a } 72° \text{ slice of the circle.}$$

15% discount on £2,300 = $\frac{15}{100} \times £2,300 = £345$

The total net amount payable is £2,300 - £345 = £1,955

Task 6

	£
List price	2,450.00
Less: discount £2,450.00 × 15/100	(367.50)
	2,082.50
Plus VAT (£2,082.50 × 20/100)	416.50
	£2,499.00

Task 7

First, you need to calculate the cost of the Effective Communication courses, so that they fit the rest of the data.

£200 × 3 days = £600   £210 × 2 ½ days = £525

Using the *mean* average:

Provider 1 = (250 + 590 + 260 + 300 + 600) ÷ 5 courses = 2,000 ÷ 5 = £400.

Provider 2 = (340 + 375 + 290 + 350 + 525) ÷ 5 courses = 1,880 ÷ 5 = £376.

Provider 2 offers the lower average course cost using this method.

Using the *median* average:

Provider 1 = 250   260   300   590   600   The median is 300.

Provider 2 = 290   340   350   375   525   The median is 350.

Provider 1 offers the lower average course cost using this method, reflecting the fact that some of Provider 1's courses are significantly cheaper than any of Provider 2's: its mean average cost is 'skewed' by the high cost of two of its courses.

Task 8

	Travel expense	%
	£	
Anne	45	15.358
Jaitinder	71	24.232
Benjamin	86	29.352
Chloe	32	10.922
Vimal	59	20.137

CHAPTER 5   Presenting information

Task 1

Email policies are often in place to avoid abuse of work time and resources (eg by using email for personal messages). They recognise that organisations may be held liable for offensive, defamatory or illegal messages by their employees, and therefore seek to ensure that no such messages are sent. They seek to preserve confidentiality and data protection, by emphasising that email is not a secure medium. They also seek to maintain a consistent organisational image, by enforcing the use of standard stationery and 'signature blocks' giving the name of the organisation and other relevant information.

Task 2

Product	Jan £000	Feb £000	Mar £000	Apr £000	May £000	Jun £000	Total £000
A	800	725	725	400	415	405	3,470
B	210	210	180	150	175	160	1,085
C	25	50	60	95	125	140	495
Total	1,035	985	965	645	715	705	5,050

(b) We'd recommend a line graph.

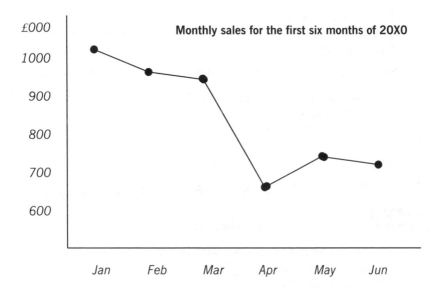

(c) We'd recommend a pie chart.

Product A:

3,470/5,050 × 100 = 68.71% =

approximately 7/10 of the circle

Product B:

1,085/5,050 × 100 = 21.49% =

approximately 1/5 of the circle

Product C:

495/5,050 × 100 = 9.8% =

Approximately 1/10 of the circle

Proportion of six months' sales

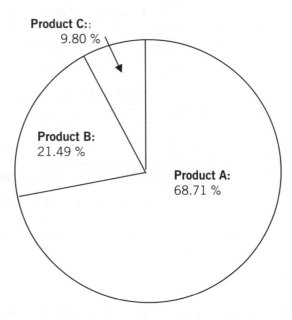

Task 3

    (a)   Dear Sirs….. Yours faithfully,
    (b)   Dear Ms Brown…. Yours sincerely,
    (c)   Dear Mark…. Kind regards,
    (d)   Dear Sir Joshua…. Yours sincerely,

Note that (d) is a special case when it is appropriate to use the person's first name in a formal address. It applies to people with the titles Sir X or Lady Y.

Task 4

    (a)   'Following our telephone conversation of [date], I enclose the brochure you requested, which details our services.'

    (b)   'I have been asked by my colleague, George Brown, to contact you in regard to your enquiry about career opportunities in the accounts department of our firm.'

    (c)   'I look forward to meeting you to discuss the matter in more detail.'

    (d)   'If you require any further information, please do not hesitate to telephone me on the number given above.'

Task 5

 SOUTHFIELD ELECTRONICS LTD

MEMORANDUM

To: Jenny Faulkner, Financial Accountant
From: Your Name, Accounts Clerk
Date: 11 September 20X0
Subject   Project re abuse of telephone procedures

I would be very pleased to take on the project of investigating ways to minimise further telephone cost increases. Thank you for the opportunity. I will have to check with Kellie, Ron and Jane, to ensure that there is sufficient flexibility in my workload, but I cannot see that this will be a problem.

My initial thoughts are that we should seek:

(a)   To disconnect handsets that we do not need
(b)   To include telephone usage in the forthcoming briefing on compliance with policy
(c)   To gain some control over staff phone usage, by using a central switchboard or call logging. With your permission, I will start by getting some information about the possibilities from an office equipment provider.

I will keep you informed as the investigation progresses.

YN

SOUTHFIELD ELECTRONICS LTD
Tomorrow's technology for today's homes

Micro House
Newtown Technology Park
Innovation Way
Middx NT3 OPN

The Sales Manager
TeleComs Ltd
6 Park Way
Brighton
Sussex BN3 4PW   11 September 20X0

Dear Sirs,

Electronic switchboards and call logging devices

I am writing to request information about your models of electronic switchboards and call logging devices, their capabilities and costs.

Southfield Electronics operates a fairly large office, and we are looking to control telephone costs. One of the approaches we will be considering is the monitoring and controlling of outgoing calls. You will no doubt be able to recommend suitable systems for our needs.

In the first instance, please send your information brochure to the office address supplied above. Alternatively, you can send material via email on: yname@southfield.co.uk.

Thank you for your attention. I look forward to hearing from you soon.

Yours faithfully,

Your Name

Your Name

Accounts Clerk

Task 6

EMAIL
Date: [inserted automatically]
To: yourname@southfield.co.uk
From: alaval@southfield.co.uk
Subject: RE: Customer analysis
Attach: customeranalysis.xls
Your name,
I attach an example of a completed customer analysis, as you requested. You will see that it is an Excel file, as I have formatted the analysis as a spreadsheet.
If you need any other help, let me know.
Amy

CHAPTER 6   Working independently

Task 1

Routine tasks are the general everyday tasks that form the basis of an employee's job. Examples in an accounts department might be producing sales invoices each day and preparing a sales ledger control account reconciliation each month.

Unexpected tasks are other duties that an employee is required to perform in addition to routine tasks. Examples might include preparing figures for a special project or performing the tasks of another employee who is on holiday.

Task 2

Urgent tasks are those for which there is an imminent deadline. For example, producing a schedule of product costings for the production manager for a meeting this afternoon or completing a report which is required for the chief accountant tomorrow morning.

Important tasks are tasks which have significant potential impacts on task fulfilment, other employees or the organisation. For example, the checking of purchase invoices to goods received notes and (perhaps counter to what you may think) the opening of the morning post.

Task 3

Clearly, without staying in the office until about 7.00 pm it will not be possible to print both the sales invoices and the report. You might consider completing the sales invoice print run and then setting up the report print and leaving the office until Monday morning. However, as the report is confidential, it would not be advisable to leave it unattended.

Both tasks are urgent but the sales invoices are *more* urgent, as they must be sent out today. The report is not needed until 12.00 noon on Monday, so provided that you make sure you can start the print run by 9.00 am on Monday, and agree this with your supervisor, this is probably the best plan of action.

Task 4

The urgent task of producing the statement must be carried out first of all as, given the meeting at 3.00 pm, the accounts assistant cannot run the risk of missing the post deadline at 4.00 pm. It would probably also be advisable to produce the list of account balances for her colleague early in the day so that it is definitely done and not forgotten. Thereafter, the routine tasks should be carried out with the meeting at 3.00 pm scheduled in.

Task 5

The furniture-maker is ahead of schedule in producing the table, having already completed it, even though it was not scheduled for completion until the end of today (Thursday). They are on schedule with the bed, having completed it as planned by the end of Wednesday. However, they are now behind schedule on the shelves, since progress is 'behind' where it should be at the 'time now' line. It may be possible to catch up, since the table-maker has spare time to help out the shelf-maker. The kitchen units aren't due to be started until tomorrow.

Task 6

TIMETABLE					
	Mon 8	Tues 9	Wed 10	Thurs 11	Fri 12
[8.00 – 9.00]	EF2	CD1	AB1	AB2	Train
9.00 – 10.00	EF2	EF1	AB1	AB3	Train
10.00 – 11.00	EF2	EF1	AB1	AB3	Train
11.00 – 12.00	EF2	EF1	AB1	AB3	Train
12.00 – 13.00					
13.00 – 14.00	CD1	EF1	AB1	AB3	Train
14.00 – 15.00	CD1	EF1	AB2	AB3	Train
15.00 – 16.00	CD1	EF1	AB2	AB3	AB4
16.00 – 17.00	CD1	AB1	AB2	AB3	AB4
[17.00 – 18.00]	CD1	AB1	AB2	AB3	AB4

Tasks carried over to week beginning 15 October:

❑ AB4 (9 hours remaining): Monday 15th

❑ AB5 (2 hours): fit in some time during this week or following

Problem tasks:

- AB2: asked for by end of the day Wednesday, but if I work early overtime, I should be able to complete the task by 9.00 am Thursday: check with AB that this is acceptable.

- AB4: asked for by end of the day Monday 15th, with nine hours remaining. May not be possible to allocate all nine hours of Monday 15th to this task: need to discuss with AB.

If AB's deadlines are not moveable, I would have to discuss the other tasks with CD and EF to see if there is any flexibility to fit in AB's tasks earlier.

Task 7

If you think that you will not be able to meet a deadline then you must inform the person that you are reporting to immediately, for two main reasons.

- The manager involved may be able to access resources which will mean that you can meet the deadline.

- If you are unable to meet your deadline, this may mean that the person you are providing the information for will also miss a deadline.

CHAPTER 7   Working as part of a team

Task 1

The accounts department will have the standing objective of preparing monthly cost accounts and annual financial accounts, invoicing and receiving money from customers, paying suppliers and other expenses – and so on. There are also likely to be specific targets and standards for how quickly, efficiently and accurately these tasks are carried out – which can be used for performance measurement and management.

Task 2

- The work may have to be transferred to other team members, meaning that their plans and schedules will have to be adjusted, and they will end up bearing a heavier share of the total work load.

- One person's failure to meet a deadline may, if there is little 'slack time' in a schedule, result in others failing to meet their deadlines. This causes them frustration and disruption – and may affect the team's ability to complete the whole task on time.

- Failure to 'pull one's weight' or meet agreed deadlines can have an impact on working relationships within the team. Resentment, frustration, blame and conflict may arise.

Task 3

As you are likely to have some spare time on Thursday, you should offer to help your colleague to input the figures to the computer that day. The entire project depends upon the figures being ready, and you should offer assistance to ensure that the project team meets this deadline. You might check with your departmental supervisor first, however, to ensure that she agrees this is the best use of your time.

Task 4

You have handled this situation effectively, because you have managed to respect your prior agreements and project deadlines – while still being courteous and co-operative in offering options to Ron Howard. The key points of the argument are:

- You have made prior commitments, which you wish to respect

- Breaking your prior commitments, by missing your deadline, will impact on the work of a project team

- Your prior commitment is to a manager at the same level of authority as Ron, and with the backing of a higher manager (Jenny Faulkner)

- It is not reasonable for Ron to ask you to work long overtime hours so that he can have personal time off: you have a right to say no

- Ron is still your superior, so you should be calm, respectful and co-operative in your dealings with him

- You have limited authority to propose alternative options: Ron should settle the matter with Kellie McDonald, since the real problem is between their conflicting demands.

Task 5

Win-lose: one team member gets the window desk and the other doesn't. (Result: resentment and demotivation of the 'losing' member.)

Compromise: the team members get the window desk on alternate days or weeks. (Result: half-satisfied needs.)

Win-win: what do they want the window desk for? One may want the view, the other better lighting conditions. This offers options to be explored: how else could the lighting be improved? (Result: this is an attempt to respect both members' needs, which may benefit future team work.)

CHAPTER 8   Developing skills and knowledge

Task 1

EMAIL	
From:	y.name@reeves.co.uk
To:	a.bolt@reeves.co.uk
Cc:	g.hoff@reeves.co.uk
Date:	*[Today's date]*
Re:	RE: Personal Development Plan

Thank you for your email about the cost of PDPs and training requests for the Accounts department. Mrs Hoff has asked me to reply on her behalf.

I am sure you are aware that all professional bodies require their members to keep their technical knowledge up-to-date, as a condition of membership. All members of the Accounts department are therefore bound to complete a certain number of hours of Continuing Professional Development activity, or they will not be able to continue as members of their professional body. This, in turn, would impact on their ability to perform their jobs.

Reeves Ltd will also benefit in many ways from Accounts department CPD activity, in terms of: more competent job performance; less supervision required; increased productivity; reduced risk and cost of errors and non-compliance with regulations/laws; improved staff motivation and morale; and an enhanced ability to recruit and retain professionally qualified staff.

I hope this explains the ambitious PDPs submitted by the department – and also goes some way to justify the cost and time requirements.

I would be happy to give you more information about CPD requirements, if this would be helpful.

YN.

Task 2

The answer depends on your own experience and reflection.

Note that in an assessment task, you may be given information about the job role you occupy in the case study (eg a job description and/or person specification), but you may *not* be given information about the strengths, weaknesses or career aspirations of the person you are 'playing' in the scenario. In such a case, as in this task, you will need to compare the *case study* job requirements with your own *real-life* strengths, weaknesses and career aspirations, in order to demonstrate that you can identify learning needs and formulate learning objectives.

Don't be confused by the mixing of a case study role and a real-life you: just pretend that the case study 'character' you are playing has the same knowledge, competences, strengths, weaknesses and career aspirations that you do.

Task 3

(a) On-the-job training, eg instruction and coaching by a more experienced operator.

(b) Perhaps an external course of training and education, eg by evening class or day release.

(c) Internal or external training course – however, it will be important that monitoring and evaluation takes place to ensure that the skills gained are applied in practice in the work team.

(d) Induction training: a special form of training in which the recruit is given an orientation to the workplace; introduced to line managers and colleagues; briefed on job requirements and company policies and procedures; and shown how to perform initial tasks, as a foundation for on-going learning needs analysis and development.

TEST YOUR LEARNING – ANSWERS

CHAPTER 2 The role of the financial functions

Test 1

A staff function is a role in the organisation which exists to support the functions directly involved in the primary activities of the business (the line functions): providing them with the resources, systems and information they need to perform those activities efficiently and effectively. Examples include: IT, HR, administration and accounting and finance.

Test 2

Financial accounting is mainly concerned with the processing and recording of transactions, and the production of financial statements (in compliance with detailed regulations) for users outside the business.

Management accounting is mainly concerned with the production of financial reports to assist managers in measuring performance, making decisions and running the business. This is not regulated by law: the reports are purely for internal use, and, for commercial reasons, are mostly kept strictly confidential.

Test 3

The typical tasks involved in payroll include:

- The calculation of gross pay
- The calculation of tax, National Insurance and other deductions
- Preparing payslips
- Making appropriate returns to external agencies such as HM Revenue and Customs
- Making up wages, or preparing data for direct credit (BACS)
- Distributing payslips to employees
- Preparing payroll statistics.

Test 4

High quality information should be complete, accurate and timely.

The payroll report has been carefully put together by Bill and as a result it was accurate.

He also appears to have made sure all the necessary information was included for processing of the payments. Therefore the information is complete.

However, because the report only reached Susan a day before the payment due date it is unlikely she will have time to transfer any necessary funds to the business current (bank) account if there are in fact insufficient funds available. She also has a short time to process the payments. The information was not timely because it was not delivered early enough to allow Susan to take any necessary action.

Test 5

Efficiency is about achieving objectives with the minimum use of resources (particularly minimum waste).

The financial functions have an important role in supporting efficiency, by providing information for planning (so that resources are not used thoughtlessly) and control (so that the use of resources is checked, and managers held accountable for how they are used). They provide the budgets and plans against which departmental performance can be measured, allowing managers to identify areas in which efficiency can be improved.

Test 6

The accounts department provides information to other departments about the cash flow implications of their activities. A positive cash flow balance may be essential (if cash reserves are low) to ensure that adequate funds are available at any given time to enable the organisation to pay its debts as they fall due (solvency). The accounts department provides information about debts that are owing and when they have to be paid; the availability of funds to cover debts when they fall due; and the cost of raising finance to keep the organisation solvent if necessary.

Test 7

ARE YOU BREAKING THE LAW?

It is essential that we comply with all provisions of the law and regulations relevant to our work.

- The law is there to protect people from loss and suffering, and ensure minimum acceptable standards of safety, integrity and good management.

- There may be financial penalties (eg fines or compensation) and operational penalties (eg loss of licence to operate) for non-compliance.

- Non-compliance can damage the reputation of our organisation, and its ability to attract investors, customers and staff.

- Non-compliance can lead to the burdens and costs of corrective action, and to closer scrutiny in future.

A positive record of compliance protects us, the integrity and standing of our profession – and our employers. Let's all take it seriously. Every task. Every time.

Test 8

SMITH'S CLEANING COMPANY

MEMORANDUM

To: Sue Hahn, Accounts Manager
From: Your Name, Accounts Assistant
Date: [Today's date]
Subject: Improving compliance with legal requirements

It appears that some 'short cuts' are being taken in the accounts department, in relation to compliance with legal requirements.

There are many laws which must be complied with in an accounting environment, in addition to the 'obvious' regulations on the preparation of financial records and statements. Examples include: the law on health and safety at work, data protection, equal opportunity and intellectual property protection.

The consequences for non-compliance are serious. So what can Smith's do to improve compliance? Management could:

(i)   Make all employees aware of the importance of compliance
(ii)   Brief all employees on their roles and responsibilities under the law (and update the briefings as the law changes), from the induction of new recruits onwards
(iii) Base organisational policies and procedures (and related employee training) on legal requirements
(iv)   Put in place checks and controls, to monitor and ensure compliance.

I am sure these issues will be discussed at the accounts department meeting. If you require any further information from me, please let me know.

YN.

CHAPTER 3 The organisational framework

Test 1

The chain of command is the imaginary 'line' by which authority in an organisation flows from higher levels down to lower levels. Each higher position (superior) in the chain has the authority to command the lower position (subordinate): to make plans and decisions, and to issue instructions, and expect them to be obeyed. Each subordinate has a corresponding obligation to report back to the superior, and to be accountable for how his or her instructions were carried out.

Your 'line manager' is the next person up the chain of command from you: that is your most immediate 'superior' in the organisation structure, and the person to whom you report most directly.

Test 2

Instructions, briefings, plans and decisions flow down the organisation structure.

Routine and exception reports, queries/questions and problems which cannot be handled at lower levels flow back up the organisation structure.

Test 3

Because the relocation is being managed as a cross-functional project by the Office Manager, and this task specifically relates to the project (and not to your everyday work in the accounts department), the person to report to here will be the Office Manager.

Test 4

It is important to adhere to office procedures and policies in order to: support efficient working (avoiding 'reinventing the wheel' for every task); support compliance with law and regulation (on which procedures and policies are often based); protect people (eg in the case of health, safety and security); and protect the finance, property, information and other assets of the organisation (eg in the case of financial controls and data security procedures).

Test 5

(a) In an accounts department where there are rarely any visits from non-employees, the employer may be happy for a degree of personalisation of work areas, eg the display of photographs. (However, these must be acceptable to others in the office, and create a professional appearance and environment.)

(b) In a reception area open to the public, it will be important to give the right impression of the organisation. Therefore, in order to appear professional and efficient, there may be stricter rules regarding the amount of personalisation allowed in this area.

Test 6

Possible policies include:

(a) Data on computer servers backed up daily and backups stored off site.

(b) Passwords containing both letters and numbers required to access accounting systems (and with monthly prompts to change the passwords)

(c) All computers installed with up to date anti-virus software

(d) Data and equipment not permitted to leave the work premises other than routine back ups.

Test 7

(a) This is a legitimate request from someone in a position of authority (provided that the R & D information is not flagged as 'classified', in which case authorisation may be required).

(b) This is likely to be sensitive information integral to the organisation's competitive advantage. Even if the caller *is* a journalist (and you have no way of knowing; she may be a competitor's R & D manager...), she has no right to this information, and should be politely refused.

(c) This is personal data (under the Data Protection Act) and should only be used for the purpose of making payments from the payroll. It is also highly personal and confidential information and should not be disclosed to anyone. The customer's request must be denied.

(d) As these notes have the copyright symbol on them, they must not be photocopied without written permission from the copyright owner, the rival company. This must be explained to the senior accounts assistant and you should not copy them – unless permission has been obtained.

Test 8

'Authorisations' are points in a procedure at which confirmation or permission to proceed must be obtained from an individual with appropriate authority.

'Designated signatories' are people who are authorised to sign documents (eg for authorisation purposes) or company cheques.

Such concepts are an important part of the organisation's system of controls to prevent fraud and the mismanagement of resources.

CHAPTER 4   Communication skills

Test 1

Purposes of business communication include: informing, persuading (eg as a part of negotiation), requesting (action or information), confirming and building working relationships.

Test 2

(a) Telephone, followed-up in writing if required

(b) Note or email

(c) Email or form to request dates, perhaps followed-up by face-to-face discussion or phone call if negotiation is required

(d) Letter

(e) Email or possibly a more formal report.

Test 3

Feedback is the response of a person with whom you are communicating, which indicates whether your message has (or has not) been received and understood as you intended.

It is important in enabling you to adjust your message, if necessary, in order to ensure that the message has been received, and that there are no misunderstandings.

Test 4

I would summarise 'communicating effectively, clearly and appropriately' as: using appropriate formats for the communication task; observing relevant format and house style conventions; presenting information professionally; ensuring that the content is technically correct; ensuring that the message is clearly understandable and tailored to the user's needs; projecting the appropriate corporate image; and achieving the purpose of the communication (as indicated by feedback from the recipient).

Test 5

(a) This does not look right, because it is unreasonably high for the job. If this employee received these wages every week, his or her annual salary would be over £50,000 per year.

(b) This looks reasonable for a quarter of the year. £25,000 ÷ 4 = £6,250, so the salary to date of £6,211.67 is about right.

(c) This does not look right. The employee's basic salary this month should be £1,500 (£18,000 ÷ 12): so your initial calculation only allows for £45 overtime. The overtime should be £450 (30 hours @ £15 per hour), and the gross pay total therefore £1,950. It looks as if the overtime was calculated as 3 hours, not 30 hours.

Test 6

PASS stands for 'Purpose, Audience, Structure, Style': the four elements that you need to consider when planning a message.

KISS stands for 'Keep It Short and Simple': an essential guideline for presenting information in a way that is clear, readily understandable and businesslike.

Test 7

Corporate identity is the organisation's chosen style for visual presentation. All visual expressions of the company should conform to corporate identity guidelines, in order to present a coherent and consistent image.

Corporate identity will impact on your communications if there are guidelines or rules for elements such as: the use of corporate logos, standard stationery, layouts, colours, typefaces, standard elements (such as signature blocks) and so on.

Test 8

EMAIL

To:	hgwells@retail.com
From:	acdoyle@southfield.co.uk
Date:	*[Today's date]*
Subject:	Your recent enquiry
Attach:	Sales brochure.pdf

Dear <u>Mr Wells,</u>

<u>Thank you</u> for your <u>enquiry about</u> our products. <u>I am glad</u> that you were able to come and see our display at the Home Entertainment Trade Fair, <u>and</u> <u>I would be</u> more than happy to help with further <u>information.</u>

Our <u>company is</u> one of the best in the field, and our <u>products</u> have recently <u>won</u> an award as Retail Product of the Year.

<u>I have</u> attached a brochure <u>which</u> details our full product range<u>. It</u> includes prices and terms of trade. <u>Once you have</u> received it, I will contact you to see if <u>you would</u> like to place an order.

In the meantime, <u>the sales team and I</u> are <u>available</u> to answer any questions you may have<u>. We would</u> be <u>glad</u> to hear from you.

<u>Thank you again for your enquiry.</u>

Arthur Doyle

Southfield Electronics

[NB Use the standard signature block for outgoing emails]

Arthur, I've just made a few amendments to your draft email, as you requested. For future reference:

- It is better to use a more formal style with senior individuals and new customers. Don't use first name terms unless they've asked you to. Avoid familiar expressions (like 'cheers'), and keep to a more formal written style (eg 'I have' instead of 'I've').

- In business communications, avoid text-message style abbreviations (like 'msg', 'IMHO' and 'gr8') and colloquial expressions (like 'cool').

- Remember to check your work for typos (like 'avaible') and spelling errors (like 'one' instead of 'won').

- You might want to make sure you write in full sentences (which contain a verb and end in a full stop), and look out for errors with clauses and apostrophes.

Test 9

Sales tax (VAT) in May $= \dfrac{20}{120} \times £4,580 = £763.3333333$ (rounded to £763.33)

Sales tax exclusive price in May $= £4,580 - £763.33 = £3,816.67$

There is a 3% increase in price for June so the sales tax exclusive price in June will be:

$£3,816.67 \times 103\% = £3,816.67 \times 1.03 = £3,931.1701$ (rounded to £3,931.17)

The sales tax will be 20% of this VAT exclusive price.

Sales tax on June purchase $= £3,931.17 \times 20\% = £786.234$ (rounded to £786.23)

Test 10

Percentage increase in revenue $=$

$$\frac{\left(£20,916 - £16,600\right)}{£16,600} \times 100 \quad = \quad \frac{£4,316}{£16,600} \times 100 = 0.26 \times 100 = 26\%$$

CHAPTER 5   Presenting information

Test 1

    (a)   Informal note (or telephone message pad)

    (b)   Face-to-face discussion (because of the sensitivity of the issue, and the need for interactive question and answer)

    (c)   Telephone or email

    (d)   Email

    (e)   Email, memo or informal report

Test 2

Elements of house style to look out for in an organisation's communication (and in assessment case scenarios) include:

- The style and location of the letterhead (if any)
- Whether all elements are against the left margin (fully blocked) or some elements are centred or against the right-hand margin (semi-blocked)
- Where the date, subject heading and salutation appear on the page
- Whether a standard signature block needs to be included.

Test 3

Your Name
Your Address

Jo Bloggs
3 Market Place
Shepherds Bush
London W12 1AW

[Today's Date]

Dear Jo,

<u>The use of appendices in report writing</u>

In response to your recent request for information about this, I thought you might appreciate the following key points.

The <u>purpose</u> of an appendix (or appendices) to a report is to separate out from the main body of the report any detailed data and supporting documents that might be helpful to the user, but might get in the way of the flow and conciseness of the main report.

In order to be used effectively, appendices should be limited in number, to avoid overloading the user with data. Each appendix should be numbered, and referred to clearly in the body of the report (eg 'see Appendix 1' or 'attached as Appendix 2'), so that the user can easily locate the supporting data if required.

These are very simple points, but I hope they are helpful to you.

If you want any further help with your report writing, just let me know. I'd be happy to help if I can.

Kind regards,

Your Name

Test 4

MEMO

To: Hugh Martin, Accounts supervisor

From: Anne Accountant, Accountant

Date: 20 May 20X1

Subject: £125 Bell computers overcharge for laptops (invoice LT241)

On 1 May 20X1 an order (ref NCA124) was placed for five laptop computers which have a list price of £500 each. On the same day Bill Fences, an account manager at Bell, agreed we would receive a 5% bulk discount because the order was for five or more computers. I enclose my notes from the phone call (including contact details for Bill) and a copy of the order for your information.

We received invoice LT241 (enclosed) for the computers today which shows the total cost of the laptops to be £2,500. Therefore the anticipated discount of £125 has not been applied and we should request that Bell send us a credit note for invoice LT241 and re-issue a new invoice with the discount applied.

Many thanks for dealing with this.

Anne

enc: Copies of order NCA124 and invoice LT241;
       Notes of phone call on 1 May 20X1

Test 5

EMAIL

To:	an.other@company.co.uk
From:	y.name@company.co.uk
Date:	[Today's date]
Subject:	Purchase ledger account balance

In response to your query: the balance shown for a supplier on the account in the purchase ledger (which we keep in the Accounts department) may *not* always be the same as the balance shown on the statement sent from that supplier.

There are a number of reasons for this. One possible reason is an error by either our Accounts department or the supplier's accounts department.

Another possible reason is a timing difference. The supplier may have sent us an invoice and recorded this on their statement just prior to sending it out. At the point when the statement is received, the invoice may not yet have been entered in our books. Equally, we might have made a payment to the supplier which has not yet been recorded on their statement, although it would already have been recorded in our purchase ledger account.

I hope this helps to clear up any confusion.

YN.

Test 6

REPORT ON DEPARTMENTAL EMAIL USAGE

To: Mr Czwynski, Accounts Manager
From: Your Name, Accounts Assistant
Date: Today's date

(a) (i) STATISTICS ON EMAIL USAGE

The total time spent on email by each of the departments over the past six months is as follows.

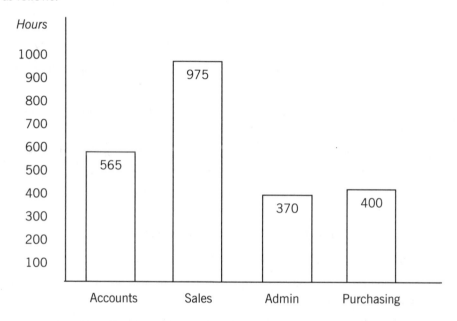

(ii)   The <u>mean average time spent on email per month by all departments</u> shows the following month-on-month trends. (For workings, see Appendix 1.)

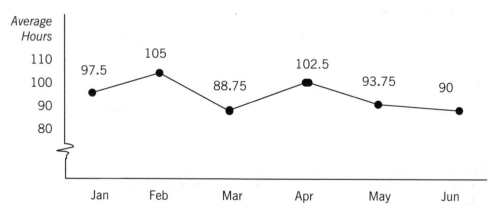

(iii)   The <u>time spent on emails per employee over six months, in each department</u> is as follows:

Accounts	565 hours ÷ 4 staff	=	141.25 hours per staff member
Sales	975 hours ÷ 5 staff	=	195 hours per staff member
Admin	370 hours ÷ 2 staff	=	185 hours per staff member
Purchasing	400 hours ÷ 2 staff	=	200 hours per staff member

From this it can be seen that although it represents a low proportion of the total number of hours spent, Purchasing has the highest usage per staff member.

(b)   RISKS AND COSTS OF ABUSE OR MISUSE OF EMAIL

Given the high degree of email usage in all departments, it is important to ensure that the email facility is used efficiently and effectively, and not abused or misused. The risks and costs of abuse or misuse of email include:

- Messages being sent to the wrong addresses, breaching confidentiality
- Messages containing offensive or otherwise illegal contents, which may make the organisation liable
- Messages containing unchecked computer viruses being sent and/or received, infecting our and others' systems
- Messages alienating current or potential customers, suppliers and business partners, due to poor style or etiquette, or virus infection
- Waste of the company's time and resources, if email is used excessively or for personal purposes.

(c)   EMAIL POLICIES THAT COULD BE IMPLEMENTED

We could implement a range of policies to control email usage, including:

- Limiting the use of office email facilities to business use (with penalties for excessive personal use)
- Making the installation and use of virus checking software mandatory
- Issuing guidelines for staff on appropriate email style, etiquette and usage
- Monitoring the content of emails to ensure proper usage
- Developing a standard 'signature block' to be appended to all external outgoing emails. (An example is attached: see Appendix 2.)

APPENDIX 1:

Workings to derive mean average hours spent on email per month

January:	(80 + 180 + 50 + 80) ÷ 4	=	97.5	hours
February:	(90 + 160 + 80 + 90) ÷ 4	=	105.0	hours
March:	(105 + 120 + 60 + 70) ÷ 4	=	88.75	hours
April:	(100 + 180 + 70 + 60) ÷ 4	=	102.5	hours
May:	(110 + 165 + 60 + 40) ÷ 4	=	93.75	hours
June:	(80 + 170 + 50 + 60) ÷ 4	=	90.0	hours

APPENDIX 2:

Specimen standard signature block for emails

[Sender's Name]
[Sender's Position]

[Company Name]
[Company Address]

[Telephone, Fax, Web contact details]

Disclaimers

This message and any attachments are confidential and may contain information that is subject to copyright. If you are not the intended recipient, please notify us immediately by replying to this message and then delete it from your system. While we take reasonable precautions to prevent computer viruses, we cannot accept responsibility for viruses transmitted to your computer and it is your responsibility to make all necessary checks. We may monitor email traffic data and the content of emails to ensure efficient operation of our business, for security, for staff training and for other administrative purposes.

CHAPTER 6   Working independently

Test 1

Urgent and important tasks

These are tasks with a close deadline and which are important to you and to other people in the organisation. For example, if you are asked to produce a report for a meeting tomorrow morning.

Urgent but not important tasks

These are tasks which are required to be done in the near future – but have no great significance. For example, replenishing the milk each morning in the office kitchen.

Not urgent but important

These are tasks which are important, but do not necessarily have to be started immediately. For example, producing a petty cash summary for the accountant by the end of the following week.

Not urgent and not important

These are tasks that are not required to be done for any particular time scale and are low priority: they can be done when you are less busy. For example, routine tasks such as packing up out-of-date files to be stored in the archives.

Test 2

Enter sales invoices/credit notes into computer system

Enter weekly purchase invoices into the computer

Match purchase invoices to goods received notes and pass to the accountant for authorisation

Filing

Test 3

1.30 to 2.30	Petty cash summary
2.30 to 2.45 (say)	Deal with petty cash claim
2.45 to 3.15	Complete petty cash summary
3.15 to 5.30	Match purchase invoices to goods received notes and pass to the accountant for authorisation
	Filing

Test 4

Thursday 31 March:	Request information from colleague
Monday 4 April and Tuesday 5 April:	Prepare report using historical information
Wednesday 6 April and Thursday 7 April:	Prepare rest of report
Friday 8 April 9.00 am to 12.00:	Print report

Test 5

An action plan is a detailed planning tool which can be used for complex projects. It is monitored on a regular basis to ensure that things are going to plan. If there are deviations from the plan then decisions are made as to how to get back on track. Information on an action plan normally includes:

- Details of each task which is part of the project
- Start date of each task
- Completion date for each task
- Person responsible for each task
- Expected and actual costs if applicable

The detailed action plan can be complex and is often used for longer term projects which need monitoring on a regular basis. In contrast a 'To Do List' is a simple short-term planning tool and consists of a checklist listing the tasks that need completing for a particular day, preferably in prioritised order. As each task is completed it is ticked off.

A 'To Do List' for the day may include a task detailed on the action plan, but will not include large long-term projects in their entirety.

Test 6

(a) On the assumption that you will want the report completed by Tuesday 21
     August the planning schedule would be as follows:

	August							
	Fri	*Mon*	*Tues*	*Wed*	*Thurs*	*Fri*	*Mon*	*Tues*
	10	*13*	*14*	*15*	*16*	*17*	*20*	*21*
Req. files	X							
Research		X	X	X				
Analysis					X	X		
Typing							X	
Proofing								X

(b) If you can't get the report typed until Tuesday 21st, you will have to
     proofread on Wednesday 22nd – and the report will be late. You must
     inform your manager immediately. She may be able to tell you that the
     report does not need to be on her desk until the end of the day. Or she
     may be able to arrange extra typing resources for the Monday.

Test 7

EMAIL

To: n.hassem@hazchem.com
From: y.name@hazchem.com
Date: [today's date]
Subject: Adhering to task deadlines

Hi, Nasif. Since you're new to the department, I thought you might appreciate some
advice on how seriously deadlines are taken here, and what to do if you encounter
problems.

Deadlines are always set for a reason: usually, because someone else needs the
information or completed work to fulfil their own task objectives. It is therefore very
important to meet agreed deadlines, so that you do not let others down, disrupt work
– and damage working relations.

If you believe that you cannot meet a specific deadline, you should immediately
inform the person who has asked you to perform the task, or your supervisor. They
may be able to change the deadline – or arrange help or additional resources so that
you can meet the original deadline.

If you need any further information about this, don't hesitate to ask me. I'd be happy
to help.

YN

Test 8

Daily tasks	Enter sales invoices into the computer
	Enter cash/cheque receipts into the computer
	Enter cash/cheque payments into computer
	Deal with petty cash claims
Weekly tasks	Enter petty cash details into the computer
	Assist in preparation of payroll
Monthly tasks	Prepare bank reconciliation

Test 9

9.00 am to 11.00 am   Enter cash/cheque receipts and payments into computer

- This is high priority, as it must be done before the bank reconciliation can be prepared

11.00 am to 12.00   Prepare sales invoice listing for the accountant

- Again, this is high priority as it is needed for a meeting at 1.00 pm

Note that the order of these two tasks could have been reversed to ensure that the accountant definitely got the figures on time.

12.00 to 1.00 pm   Lunch break

1.00 pm to 3.00 pm   Prepare bank reconciliation

- This must be completed by 5.00 pm

3.00 pm to 3.30 pm   Deal with sales representatives petty cash claims

- An unexpected task which must be fitted in at this point

3.30 pm to 4.00 pm   Deal with other petty cash claims for the day

You now have one-and-a-half hours left until the end of the day and have completed all of the tasks that must be done today. During the remainder of the day you can start on the sales invoice inputs or complete the petty cash computer entries and then move on to the sales invoice inputs with the remainder being completed on Monday.

Test 10

(a) The problem is that due to Jenny's workload, you are unable to complete your task to deadline – or to say when it might be completed. You lack the power to enforce co-operation from a member of another department. You also have the deadline imposed by Parvinder's holiday: you need to return to Accounts on the day planned.

(b) You will need to inform Mr Sproule of the problem with getting the HR information, as it is his project deadline you are in danger of missing. He may have the authority as project manager to influence the HR department.

You will need to inform Mrs Tancredi that there may be a scheduling conflict that will require you to extend your secondment in order to complete your report.

You should inform Parvinder that there may be a question mark over the date of your return to the department, so that he can make alternative arrangements to brief you, if necessary.

(c)

MEMO

To:	Mr Sproule, Project Manager
From:	Your Name, Project Team Member (Accounts)
Date:	Today's date
Subject:	Report on the employee database

I thought it advisable to inform you that I am currently experiencing some delays in accessing the information required from the HR department in order to complete my report.

With six working days remaining until the report deadline, and the end of my agreed secondment, I have been unable to obtain the information from Jenny Gomez, the HR assistant. Jenny has been unable to say when she will have time to prepare the information, despite my best efforts to impress upon her the urgency of my task.

If the information is not immediately available, my concern is that I will be unable to meet the agreed deadline for submitting the report. There is also the risk that my secondment will over-run.

May I leave it with you to contact Mrs Tancredi, and to determine what you both think best in regard to the possible prolonging of my secondment? Alternatively, I would appreciate your advice about how the Personnel Records information might be obtained more swiftly.

Thank you for your understanding.

YN

CHAPTER 7   Working as part of a team

Test 1

Receivables ledger (sales ledger) team
Payroll section
Special project team

Test 2

There are a number of advantages of working as part of a team rather than on an individual basis:

- *Additional resources*: different skills, experience and ideas which can be pooled

- *Inspiration*: the ideas and suggestions of each team member can influence the performance of the other members

- *Motivation:* the shared goals and the help and support of others can provide additional motivation to team members in their work

- *Communication:* team working is a tool of co-ordination because it provides a forum for task-related communication (particularly between different departments, eg on a project team)

Test 3

Roles that people might occupy in a team will include:
Leading the team
Generating ideas
Implementing the ideas
Maintaining the relationships between the team members

Test 4

It is highly likely that the tasks that you perform will have an effect on other team members. Information that you provide will be used by others and they may not be able to complete their tasks until you have completed yours. Therefore, schedules and timetables must be set by the team leader to ensure that there is full integration of the work of all team members. It is important that each individual meets their commitments according to the schedules set, in order for the team to achieve its objectives.

Test 5

Synergy is the concept that sometimes two heads are better than one and therefore teams can often accomplish more than the same individuals working alone.

Mutual assistance within teams can help provide synergies when one member of the team, still being able to fulfil his/her other commitments, is able to help another member struggling due to time or other restraints (for example lack of skill/experience in a particular area). This attitude is then reciprocated by the assisted team member when the roles are reversed. The overall result is that more work is completed on time and its quality is better than it may have otherwise been.

Test 6

The first course of action may be to discuss the accounts assistant's behaviour confidentially with a trusted colleague. You should then talk to the accounts assistant himself and explain your concerns. If there is no solution drawn from these discussions, your only action would be to talk to your line manager about the problem.

Test 7

If you are trying to influence someone, you will need to communicate assertively (without being aggressive) and put forward your views clearly. You will need to listen, first, to the other person, so that you can argue logically against their reasons, and can tailor your solution to their needs.

Test 8

Win-lose: one of you gets the file and the other doesn't. (Result: one party fails to meet their commitments.)

Compromise: one of you gets the file now, and the other gets it later (although this has an element of win-lose, since the other has to work late or take it home).

Win-win: you photocopy the file and *both* take it – or one of you consults his or her boss and gets an extension of the deadline (since getting the job done in time is the real aim – not just getting the file). Result: both deadlines are met, and collaboration has probably enhanced the working relationship between the colleagues.

Test 9

> Your Name
> Your Address
> Date
>
> The Editor
> *Student Accountant Magazine*
> 3 Graves St
> Bristol BR3 3NG
>
> Dear Sir,
>
> **Assertive communication**
>
> In response to a letter which appeared on your letter pages in the last issue ('Don't wipe your feet on the doormat', 23/04/X0), I would like to emphasise that standing up for your needs and rights at work is an essential part of managing a workload and working effectively in a team.
>
> Being appropriately assertive means standing up for your own rights, needs and opinions (ie not being passive or a 'doormat') – *without* dismissing the rights, needs or opinions of others (ie not being 'selfish' or 'aggressive').
>
> One has a right to say 'no' to inappropriate or unreasonable demands – as well as to bullying conduct – but one can choose to do this in a way that is calm, courteous, professional, positive and co-operative.
>
> The key is to state clearly and directly what the problem is, and what you want or do not want to happen. You can then, where possible, propose alternative solutions to meet the other person's needs – or invite them to make alternative suggestions, which you will consider positively.
>
> Assertive communication is an important skill for accountants. We may occupy a service role in the organisation – but we are not 'doormats'.
>
> Yours faithfully,
>
> *Your Name*
>
> Your Name
> Student Accountant

Test 10

Initially, you might talk to George and explain that you are happy to help out in an emergency but not to do his work for him on a day-to-day basis.

If the situation does not improve after talking to George personally, you will have to consider reporting the matter to your line manager.

Test 11

Grievances within the workplace might include:

- Sexual or racial harassment
- Unfair treatment or discrimination due to race, gender or disability
- An employee being given an unfair workload
- An employee being blocked for promotion

CHAPTER 8   Developing skills and knowledge

Test 1

Members of professional bodies are required to complete a certain amount of CPD as a condition of continuing membership. This ensures that their knowledge and skills are always up-to-date and of a good standard – which, in turn, protects the interests of their clients and employers, as well as the standing and credibility of the professional bodies and the accounting profession.

CPD activity has to be recorded in order to provide evidence that the required hours and activities have been undertaken.

Test 2

Training benefits individual employees in many ways. It can enable improved job performance, which in turn gives potential for increased rewards and recognition, greater job security, enhanced job satisfaction, and the ability to take on further challenge/responsibility in the job (ie be promoted). Learning and development can also enhance the employee's confidence, versatility and flexibility, which may in turn make him or her more valuable in the external job market (ie employability).

Test 3

Job description: a statement of the tasks and responsibilities that make up the job, together with reporting lines.

Person specification: a statement of the essential and desirable characteristics of the person the organisation is looking for in a job, or the ideal job-holder.

Test 4

EMAIL

From: yourname@stubbs.com
To: jobloggs@stubbs.com
Date: *[Today's date]*
Re: RE: Learning needs analysis

Hi, and welcome to Stubbs. There are plenty of different approaches to identifying your learning needs. Here are a few ideas to get you started.

- You can review the job description and person specification for your job (available from the HR department) and consider your current competence and qualities against the requirements set out in them. Ask yourself what your strengths and weaknesses are – or what the 'gaps' in your current competence, knowledge or qualities are. This may immediately suggest learning needs.

- You could start keeping a personal development journal, in which you record any incidents or feedback which indicate a learning need.

- You could scan the office notice board for advertised training courses that strike you as relevant to your job.

- You could ask your supervisor or colleagues for feedback on 'gaps' in your performance: 'What do you think I need to learn about or do better'?

Your supervisor should be able to steer you through these processes when you review your induction training, and identify learning needs for the future. But at least you will have got a head start on thinking about it.

If you want any more help, let me know.

YN

Test 5

Specific	Development objectives must be specific rather than general
Measurable	In order to be able to evaluate progress, objectives must be formulated such that the achievement of them can be measured
Agreed	Personal development objectives will often require significant resources from the employer and therefore must be agreed with the appropriate manager
Realistic	To avoid frustration and failure, objectives must be realistic or achievable using available time and other resources
Time-bounded	Objectives must be set within a specific time scale

Test 6

Examples include (only four were required):

Courses	Internal or external educational or training courses
Journals/trade publications	Technical information and updates (and training/educational opportunities)
Books	Technical and educational material
Colleagues	Learning skills, methods and techniques from colleagues on a formal or informal basis
Observation	A method of learning by observing how colleagues or superiors carry out their tasks

Test 7

Popular search engines are often used together with key words to find web pages with details of the laws and regulations you are looking for. However, those websites listed first may not be the most reliable websites if they are not provided by a recognised or reliable source. They may therefore not be up to date or may contain inaccuracies. This can have an impact on the individual using the information as they may rely on, or pass on, this incorrect information in their role as a professional.

In order to make sure the information being learned from is accurate the integrity of the provider should be verified. Sometimes you are able to check the last date the page was updated to ensure it is up to date information and this should be checked wherever possible.

Test 8

(a) Internet research (or checking the corporate library of technical updates and bulletins)

(b) Using a textbook, or applying for a training course, if (s)he has no prior knowledge. If (s)he has already learned the basics, but lacks confidence or is not yet fully competent, (s)he might seek out a more expert colleague to act as 'coach': instructing, demonstrating and giving supervised opportunities to practice.

(c) In this situation, the best approach may be experiential learning. The employee may seek out opportunities to participate in meetings, and try out new behaviours: asking more questions, or stating an opinion more assertively, or volunteering to take notes of the meeting. Feedback should then be sought from fellow participants, to gauge whether the new behaviours were successful – or need to be adjusted further next time. And so on, in an ongoing learning cycle.

Test 9

You can compare your own progress against your PDP goals on a regular basis. (Have you attained the targets you set?)

Another review method is to get informal feedback from your supervisor or colleagues. (How do they think you have improved – and could improve still further?)

Most organisations plan periodic progress reviews (especially in project work and for new recruits).

There will also probably be annual PERFORMANCE APPRAISAL for all employees.

Test 10

A performance appraisal might cover:

- Review of work performance since last appraisal
- Feedback on strengths, weaknesses and improvement/learning needs
- Review of progress towards meeting objectives set at last appraisal
- Setting of new objectives for next period

AAT SAMPLE ASSESSMENT

Scenario

Today's date is Friday 2nd July 20X0 and you (Sam Barnes) started working as a financial accounts clerk for Debson's Drinks on Monday 8th June.

The Accounts department is split into two distinct sections:

- Financial accounts where the nominal ledger, sales ledger, purchases ledger and taxation records are maintained; and

- Management accounts where the stocks, and the regional management accounting records are maintained.

Your normal working week is 9 am to 5 pm, and you are required to take one hour for lunch. During the busy weeks of the year end, everyone is expected to work longer to complete work. However, the offices are only open between the hours of 8 am and 6 pm.

Please refer to the next page for the organisational chart of the Accounts department of Debson's Drinks.

Your role is primarily to assist with the maintenance of the nominal ledger, and most of your tasks are routine. However, when you joined Debson's Drinks, Carol Nixon explained that as a financial accounts clerk, you are to be a shared resource between all four of the assistant financial accountants, and therefore you may be asked to complete tasks by any of these sections.

As your job is a new role within Debson's Drinks, Carol is unsure how it will work having four assistant financial accountants allocating you tasks, and so she has asked you to keep your work request forms and work plans to review with her at your three month review. Carol has explained that the assistant financial accountants will complete a work request form, which is to be received by 10 am each Friday for work to be completed the following week. This will enable you to plan your forthcoming workload and identify any issues before the new week starts.

ORGANISATIONAL CHART OF DEBSON'S DRINKS LTD

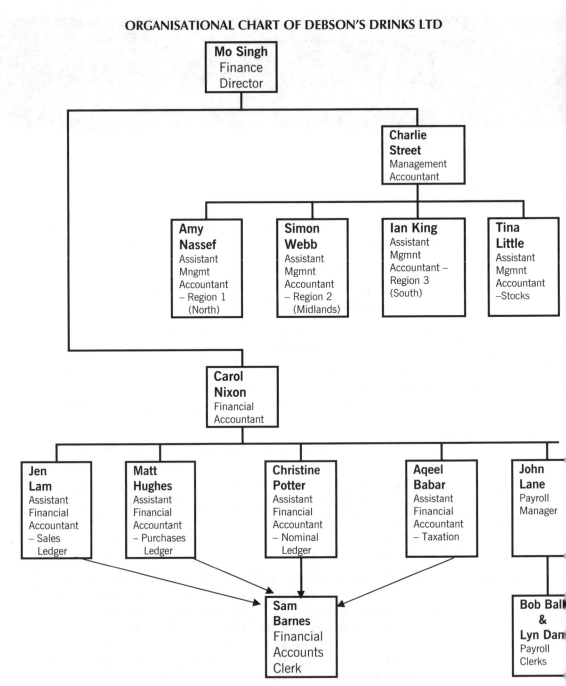

Carol Nixon reviews all staff training and development for the Financial Accounts department, and she has authorised the payment of your AAT course fees. The Human Resources manager, Sally Green, has received and processed the payment but is rather unhappy about the total cost of training for the Financial Accounts department staff.

During your first four weeks in the job, you completed a generic one-week induction to Debson's Drinks. Your departmental induction has mainly been with Christine

Potter, going through the workings of the nominal ledger and the routine tasks you will be required to complete on a monthly basis. Unfortunately, Debson's year-end date is 30th June and therefore everyone in the Accounts department is extremely busy. Christine explained that she would be asking you to do tasks which she would not have the time to explain fully. However, you should keep a list of anything you don't understand and she would set aside time after the year-end to go through everything with you.

ORGANISATIONAL POLICY – EXPENSE CLAIMS FORMS (SALES)

All expense claim forms must be accompanied by VAT receipts in support of amounts claimed by employees. Claim forms must be completed and sent to the respective authorising manager by 4th of each month. The authorising manager must authorise the claims (up to their limits) and send to the Accounts department by 10th of each month. The Accounts department will process all correctly completed claims and include the payment in that month's salary. If any aspect of the claim is incorrect the form is returned to the authorising manager and the payment of the money will be delayed by at least one month.

Authority limits per period:

- Regional Sales Managers can authorise total claims for their own sales team up to a total of £200 (per team member).

- All monthly claims of £200 or more must be authorised by the Sales Director, Tom Ford.

You have received the following work request forms by 10 am today:

WORK REQUEST FORM			**Date:** 2nd July 20X0
FOR: Sam Barnes			
FROM: Chris Potter			
Code	**Task**	**Estimated Duration**	**Required @ close of business**
CP 1	Complete Journals for the year-end accruals	7 hours	7th July
CP 2	Analyse the prepayments and provide report	5 hours	7th July
CP 3	Action the management accounts adjustments as per the list attached	8 hours	8th July
CP 4	Reconcile the Fixed Assets accounts (cost and accumulated depreciation) with the nine fixed asset registers. Highlight any inconsistencies	12 hours	12th July
CP 5	Reconcile the stock figures with the attached lists from management accounts	6 hours	9th July
CP 6	Collect money from everyone in the Accounts department for a present for Lyn Dan's wedding.	2 hours	23rd July

WORK REQUEST FORM		**Date:** 2nd July 20X0	
FOR: Sam Barnes			
FROM: Matt Hughes			
Code	Task	Estimated Duration	Required @ close of business
MH1	Match supplier statements to the Purchases Ledger balances and highlight any differences	6 hours	6th July

WORK REQUEST FORM		**Date:** 2nd July 20X0	
FOR: Sam Barnes			
FROM: Jen Lam			
	Task	Estimated Duration	Required @ close of business:
JL1	Contact the attached five debtors requesting payment ASAP – update debtor records, recording the outcome of the conversation	6 hours	6th July
JL2	Complete the banking documentation for the attached cheques received from debtors	4 hours	5th July

Carol Nixon has also provided you with the following CPD requests for the next financial year.

CPD request for the Financial Year ending 30 June 20X1				
Name	**Event/Course**	**Provider**	**Duration**	**Cost**
Jen Lam	ATT qualification	National Training College (NTC)	1 day per month	£2,000
	Credit Management	Local Branch Event	1 evening – 3 hours	Free
	VAT Update	HMRC	1 day	Free
	Legal Compliance	Local Branch Event	1 day	£250
	Managing People	Local Branch Event	1 evening – 3 hours	Free
Matt Hughes	Legal Compliance	Local Branch Event	1 day	£250
	VAT Update	HMRC	1 day	Free
Chris Potter	International Accounting Standards Update	CIMA	1 day	£400
	CIMA final level qualification	NTC	1 day per month for 12 months	£2,000
	Effective delegation techniques	CMI	1 day	£300
Aqeel Babar	CTA qualification	NTC	1 day per month for 12 months	£3,500
	VAT Update	HMRC	1 day	Free
	Corporation Tax Update	HMRC	1 day	Free
	Income Tax Update	HMRC	1 day	Free
	Online reporting	HMRC	1 day	Free
John Lane	AAT Level 4 Diploma in Accounting	NTC	1 afternoon each week for 35 weeks	£1,850
Sam Barnes	AAT Level 2 Certificate in Accounting	NTC	1 afternoon each week for 35 weeks	£1,050
Bob Ball	HMRC Payroll Update	HMRC	1 day	Free
Lyn Dan	HMRC Payroll Update	HMRC	1 day	Free

Estimated organisational cost in overtime in covering the work of those whom are attending formal training:

- Assistant Financial Accountant/Payroll Manager grade – £50 per half day
- Accounts Assistant/Clerk grade – £30 per half day

JOB DESCRIPTION	
POST DETAILS	
Job Title	Financial Accounts Assistant
Salary	£11,500 – 13,500
Location	Northampton Depot
Reports to	Carol Nixon
Date	March 20X0

KEY RESPONSIBILITIES

- To undertake the day-to-day functions of the accounts department including taking messages, dealing with enquiries by telephone from customers and suppliers.
- To use own initiative to deal with and react to enquiries in the absence of an Assistant Financial Accountant.
- To provide administrative and clerical support to the Assistant Financial Accountants, including filing, answering the telephone and dealing with the post.
- To undertake work as requested by the Assistant Financial Accountants.
- To be aware of the importance of maintaining strict confidentiality in all aspects of work.

PERSON SPECIFICATION		
CRITERIA	**ESSENTIAL**	**DESIRABLE**
Qualifications	■ GCSE English Language (Grade A* – C) ■ GCSE Mathematics (Grade A* – C)	Undertaking AAT Level 2 qualification Willingness to undertake higher level study Level 2 Word processing Level 2 Spreadsheets
Experience	■ Evidence of good organisational skills ■ Basic computer skills ■ General office procedures	Previous accounts or clerical experience
Communication skills	■ Ability to communicate effectively in a range of situations ■ Evidence of successfully communicating with people at all levels ■ Understanding of confidentiality	
Team work	■ Knowledge and understanding of working in a team ■ Ability to work flexibly in a team	Previous experience of working in a team

TASK 1.1a

You have been provided with information about the accounts department of Debson's Drinks, but they do not work in isolation. Explain:

(i)   One example of information which the Accounts department (either Management or Financial Accounts) will receive from other departments

(ii)   One example of information which the Accounts department will provide to other department(s).

TASK 1.1b

Explain how the information provided by the Accounts department will help Debson's Drinks become more efficient and maintain its solvency.

TASK 1.1c

All organisations must operate within a legal framework, and the consequences of non-compliance are heavy fines or even imprisonment. Considering the Accounts department environment, explain how it can ensure it complies with legal requirements and provide two examples of specific areas which are covered by legislation.

TASK 1.1d

Your role is to support all of the Financial Accounts section and you are required to work for all four assistant financial accountants. Therefore, you do not have requests for work from just one person. Identify to whom you would refer the following working issues.

(i)   You have received incomplete information for a Nominal ledger task
(ii)   You have concerns about your AAT studies

TASK 1.1e

You have been completing a task reviewing sales staff expense claims, and you notice that a number of these have been authorised by a Regional Manager for amounts which are higher than £200 per team member. Complete an e-mail to Carol suitable for her to issue to the Sales departments, explaining why it is important for the sales managers to authorise expense claim forms correctly, and the consequences if they are incorrectly authorised.

EMAIL	
From:	s.barnes@Debsons.com
To:	c.nixon@Debsons.com
Date:	
Subject:	

TASK 1.2a

By 10 am on Friday 2nd July you have received the work request forms reproduced in the scenario. Please review these and complete the work schedule below, indicating the task to be completed for each hour of each working day. You are also required to identify any task(s) where you may have difficulty in meeting the deadlines requested, and any tasks which you will carry forward to week commencing 12th July.

WORK PLAN					
	Monday 5th July	Tuesday 6th July	Wednesday 7th July	Thursday 8th July	Friday 9th July
Possible 8 – 9					
9 – 10					
10 – 11					
11 – 12					
LUNCH 12 – 13					
13 – 14					
14 – 15					
15 – 16					
16 – 17					
Possible 17 – 18					

TASK 1.2b

Just before you leave at 5 pm, Aqeel comes to you asking you to do a task for him first thing on Monday morning. He estimates it will take no longer than three hours to complete, but it would enable him to finish work early and collect his children from school. Aware that you have just completed the work plan for the next week and you have no spare time, you are concerned about this request. Explain how and when you will explain to Aqeel that you are unable to complete the work and the consequences to your other work (and therefore other assistant financial accountants) if you complete this work for him.

TASK 1.2c

Aqeel is not happy that you are unable to do his three hour task and feels that as this is the only task he is requesting next week, you should treat this as a priority. Explain how you would deal with this to try to resolve the situation and what you would do if you were unable to resolve the issue.

SECTION 2

TASK 2.1a

All of the accounts staff are members of either one of the Chartered Accountancy bodies or the AAT. Write a letter to Sally Green, who is based at Debson's Head Office (Debson's House, Orchard Business Park, Milton Keynes, MK1 2XY), explaining why the training for accounts staff is required by these professional bodies, and why it is important to maintain CPD.

Debson's Drinks Ltd
Distribution Depot
Units 10-25 North Road
Northampton NN1 5XR

2nd July 20X0

TASK 2.1b

In the scenario, you have been provided with the CPD requests for 20X1 for the Financial Accounts section of the Accounts department.

You are required to calculate the total cost to be paid to the training provider(s) for each member of staff, and also the total cost of the training – including the cost to the organisation in covering the work while trainees are away from work. You are also required to calculate the costs for each employee as a percentage (to 2 decimal places) of the total cost of CPD for the Financial Accounts section.

TASK 2.1c

Review the Job description and person specification for your job against your skills and identify two strengths and two weaknesses you possess.

STRENGTHS	WEAKNESSES
1.	1.
2.	2.

TASK 2.1d

Focusing on the weaknesses identified in Task 2.1c, the current requirements in the job description and person specification and your future career aspirations, identify at least four further development needs using the Personal Development Plan (PDP) pro forma on the following page.

PERSONAL DEVELOPMENT PLAN FOR THE FORTHCOMING YEAR

Name: _____

Date: _____

What do I want/ need to learn?	What will I do to achieve the learning need?	What resources or support will I need?	Target date for completion	With whom and when will this be reviewed?
1. AAT Level 2 Cert. in Accounting	Attend my training provider	Time to revise for my exams	April 20X1	Carol Nixon at 3 month review
2.				
3.				
4.				
5.				
6.				
7.				

TASK 2.1e

As Sam Barnes, you have been asked to write a short report (no more than one page) to Carol Nixon reviewing your first month at Debson's Drinks.

You are required to include the following sections in the report:

- Review of first month – provide a brief overview of your first month as detailed in the scenario provided.

- Difficulties – identify any difficulties that you think Sam Barnes may have encountered during the first month working for Debson's Drinks.

- How I produced my PDP – explain the process you went through to identify your strengths and weaknesses in Task 2.1c, and include reference to any documents you used to analyse your strengths and weaknesses.

- Monitoring my PDP – having completed your PDP in Task 2.1d, explain why it is important to review this on a regular basis.

You are required to include suitable closing comments and to attach your PDP as an appendix to your report.

REPORT on _____

TO: _____

FROM: _____

DATE: _____

AAT SAMPLE ASSESSMENT – ANSWERS

TASK 1.1a

Information the Accounts department receives

The Accounts department will receive information from all other departments of the organisation such as production schedules, expense claim forms, salary and overtime hours, changes to staff details, invoices to process and pay, etc.

Information the Accounts department provides

The Accounts department will provide information to the sales department on customer debts, current costs against the expected budgeted costs, depreciation charges, expenses, etc.

TASK 1.1b

The Accounts department will provide information on all financial aspects of the business and as such it provides other parts of the business with information on how their area or department is performing which should enable the department to focus on how efficiently it is running and possible areas where efficiency can be improved.

The Accounts department will also produce the annual budgets and long-term plans in conjunction with other department managers. During the year the Accounts department will provide all areas of the organisation with current figures as compared to the budgeted figures which will serve as a benchmark.

The Accounts department will provide the Sales department with information on debtors and, through a strict credit control policy, will ensure the cash balances of the business are closely monitored and therefore solvency is assured.

TASK 1.1c

It is important that Debson's Drinks and all its employees are aware of the legal requirements. All employees must be briefed on their roles and responsibilities. The legal framework will include rules on Health and Safety, Data Protection, employment conditions and law, corporate requirements etc.

TASK 1.1d

(i)   As this is specifically a Nominal Ledger task, I would refer the problem to Chris Potter.

(ii)   As Carol Nixon is responsible for monitoring my personal development and training, issues with my AAT studies would be referred to her.

TASK 1.1e

E-MAIL

From:	s.barnes@Debsons.com
To:	c.nixon@Debsons.com
Date:	2 July 20X0
Subject:	Expense claim forms

Hello, Carol.

Please find the information below which I think should be passed on to the team to clarify the policy.

Since I have lately received a number of incorrect expense claim forms, I would ask you to consider the following before submitting your expense claim forms to the Accounts department.

- All expense claim forms must be fully and legibly completed.

- All claims for expenses must be accompanied by a VAT receipt.

- All claims must be with the authorising manager by the 4th of each month.

- For total claims up to £200 in the period, your claim is to be authorised by your Regional Sales Manager.

- For total claims exceeding £200 in the period, your claim should be sent to Tom Ford, Sales Director.

Authorising managers must ensure the correctly completed and authorised claim forms are with the Accounts department by 10th of each month for the claim to be paid in that month's salary run.

Unfortunately, incorrectly completed – and incorrectly authorised – claim forms have to be returned to the originator and this will result in a delay in the claimant receiving their monies.

Sam Barnes

TASK 1.2a

WORK PLAN					
	Monday 5th July	Tuesday 6th July	Wednesday 7th July	Thursday 8th July	Friday 9th July
Possible 8 – 9	JL2	MH1	CP1	CP2	CP5
9 – 10	JL2	JL1	CP1	CP3	CP5
10 – 11	JL2	JL1	CP1	CP3	CP5
11 – 12	JL2	JL1	CP1	CP3	CP5
LUNCH 12 – 13					
13 – 14	MH1	JL1	CP1	CP3	CP5
14 – 15	MH1	JL1	CP2	CP3	CP5
15 – 16	MH1	JL1	CP2	CP3	CP4
16 – 17	MH1	CP1	CP2	CP3	CP4
Possible 17 – 18	MH1	CP1	CP2	CP3	CP4

If I worked from 8 am to 6 pm every day, then I anticipate two problems, both with Chris Potter's tasks (CP2 and CP4). They are asked for by the close of business, but I could complete them by 9 am the following day. This would need to be discussed with Chris and, if this is not acceptable, then I would have to discuss the other tasks with Jen and Matt to see if there is any flexibility on completion dates.

To Do List: week commencing 12th July

- **CP4** – 12 hours work to be completed by the end of Monday 12th July. I plan to complete 3 hours on Friday and if I work when the office is open on Monday and Tuesday, I can have the work completed for 9 am on Tuesday 13th July. – *Need to discuss with Chris Potter*

- **CP6** – 2 hours to be completed by 23rd July: should be able to fit this in with my workload.

TASK 1.2b

I would speak with Aqeel as soon as possible and show him my work plan as evidence of my current workload. I would speak with Aqeel courteously and with respect, but explain that I will be unable to complete the work as things stand at the moment, and that I am already planning to work overtime to complete the tasks I currently have to complete. It should be explained that if this job were accepted, it would mean that a number of other jobs would be delayed and their respective deadlines would be missed.

TASK 1.2c

Speak calmly but emphasise that Aqeel is at the same level of seniority as Chris Potter, Matt Hughes and Jen Lam, all of whom would be affected if this additional task is accepted. Maybe involve them in a discussion to see if there is any flexibility on the deadlines to enable me to complete the extra work from Aqeel. If this does not resolve the issue, as Carol Nixon is the direct line manager, she should be involved in discussions to help find a satisfactory solution.

SECTION 2

TASK 2.1a

Debson's Drinks Ltd
Distribution Depot
Units 10-25 North Road
Northampton NN1 5XR

2nd July 20X0

Sally Green, HR Manager
Debson's Drinks Ltd
Debson's House
Orchard Business Park
Milton Keynes MK1 2XY

Dear Sally

CPD for Accounting Professional Bodies

All professional bodies require their members to ensure that their technical knowledge is up-to-date, as a condition of membership. This is achieved through continuing professional development (CPD), which can take a number of forms but commonly includes some form of formal training. All members of the accounts department at Debson's Drinks are members of one or other of the professional accountancy bodies and are therefore required to complete CPD.

Debson's Drinks also benefits from this, as it can be assured that its employees' knowledge is up-to-date, thus minimising the chance of their work not meeting regulatory standards. CPD also increases employees' knowledge of new areas, from which again Debson's will benefit, as they may be able to undertake further work.

I hope this explains the need for formal training by the Accounts department, but do not hesitate to contact me if I can be of further help.

Yours sincerely

Sam Barnes

Sam Barnes
Financial Accounts Clerk

Name	Event/Course	Duration	Cost	Org cost to cover	Total cost per employee	% total cost
Jen Lam	ATT qualification	1 day per month (=12 days)	£2,000	£1,200	£3,650	19.09
	Credit Management	1 evening – 3 hours	Free	0		
	VAT Update	1 day	Free	£100		
	Legal Compliance	1 day	£250	£100		
	Managing People	1 evening – 3 hours	Free	0		
Matt Hughes	Legal Compliance	1 day	£250	£100	£450	2.35
	VAT Update	1 day	Free	£100		
Chris Potter	International Accounting Standards Update	1 day	£400	£100	£4,100	21.44
	CIMA final level qualification	1 day per month (= 12 days)	£2,000	£1,200		
	Effective delegation techniques	1 day	£300	£100		
Aqeel Babar	CTA qualification	1 day per month (=12 days)	£3,500	£1,200	£5,100	26.67
	VAT Update	1 day	Free	£100		
	Corporation Tax Update	1 day	Free	£100		
	Income Tax Update	1 day	Free	£100		
	Online reporting	1 day	Free	£100		
John Lane	AAT Level 4 Diploma in Accounting	1 afternoon per week – 35 weeks (35 × 50)	£1,850	£1,750	£3,600	18.83
Mary Brown	AAT Level 2 Certificate in Accounting	1 afternoon per week - 35 weeks (35 × 50)	£1,050	£1,050	£2,100	10.98
Bob Ball	HMRC Payroll Update	1 day	Free	£60	£60	0.31
Lyn Dan	HMRC Payroll Update	1 day	Free	£60	£60	0.31
Totals:			11,600	7,520	19,120	–

TASK 2.1c

The candidate should assess their own real-life skills against those identified in the person specification and also the requirements of the job description.

<u>STRENGTHS</u>	<u>WEAKNESSES</u>
1.	1.
2.	2.

TASK 2.1d

Candidates are required to make sensible suggestions related to the current role as Financial Accounts Clerk as described and also their own (real life) career aspirations. Timescales should also be considered.

TASK 2.1e

REPORT on Sam Barnes' PDP and monitoring

TO: Carol Nixon

FROM: Sam Barnes

DATE: 2nd July 20X0

1 Review of my first month

I have now been working for Debson's for four weeks: only three of those weeks have been spent in the Accounts department, as my first week was spent completing the organisation's induction course. I have spent most of my time with Chris Potter, covering the basics of the nominal ledger and the routine tasks I will be required to do every period.

During the last week or so, everybody has been very busy preparing for the year-end, so I have been instructed to work things out for myself and ask when I encounter difficulties.

2 Difficulties

Ideally, I would have liked to have had more time to work with the systems and procedures before the busy year-end period. However, I believe that once I have completed the year-end workload, I will have a much better understanding of the systems. Chris has advised me to make a list of everything I do not understand, and we can go through this list when the year-end has been completed.

I have had difficulties in that the work requests by the assistant financial accountants have exceeded the number of hours I am able to work (taking into account office opening hours). I have, as instructed, retained the work request forms and my work plans, so that the situation can be reconsidered at my three-month review meeting.

3 How I produced my PDP

I assessed my strengths and weaknesses against the Job Description and Person Specification supplied, to identify areas where I need to develop further. Having assessed these, I was able to focus on areas of weakness to produce the attached PDP (Appendix 1).

4 Importance of monitoring my PDP

As I am very new to Debson's Drinks, I am not sure of the procedures for PDP monitoring, but I do understand that it is important for us to agree this plan and also to monitor my progress on a regular basis, to ensure that my development is progressing in line with what you expect of me.

I hope that this short report is useful to you, and that we can discuss the contents further when we have my three-month review meeting.

Appendices:

Appendix 1: PDP (attached)

Scenario

You have been working for Badders UK Ltd for nearly a year now as a management accounts clerk. You work for the assistant management accountant and she works for the management accountant called Jo Potter. Your friend is a financial accounts clerk and he works for the assistant financial accountant, who works for the financial accountant called Lesley Snape. Jo and Lesley report to the financial director called Sam Longbottom.

You work in the Nuneaton office which covers the sales of badminton racquets in the Warwickshire region. Occasionally you need to visit the warehouse in Coventry to help with the stock take (inventory count).

Your normal working week is 8 am to 4 pm, and you are required to take one hour for lunch. During the busy weeks of the year end, everyone is expected to work longer to complete work. However, the offices are only open between the hours of 8 am and 7 pm.

Your role is primarily to assist with the preparation of the stock (inventory) reports and the maintenance of the fixed asset register (non-current asset register) and most of your tasks are routine. However, when you joined Badders UK Ltd, the management accountant explained that you may have to help out with other areas of the business if people were on holiday or off sick. So far you have had no experience of the payroll department but you have covered for the financial accounts clerk when he has been off sick.

INFORMATION POLICY

- Personal data must be accurate.
- Personal data must only be kept for as long as necessary.
- Personal data must be kept securely.
- No information about customers or employees must be revealed to other customers or employees

---

You have received the following work request forms by 10 am today:

WORK REQUEST FORM	Date: 2nd July 20X0
FOR: Management accounts clerk	
FROM: Assistant financial accountant	

Code	Task	Estimated Duration	Required
CP 1	Complete the banking documentation for the attached cheques received from receivables (debtors) and visit the bank.	3 hours	Friday before bank closes at 12.00

WORK REQUEST FORM		Date: 2nd July 20X0	
FOR: Management accounts clerk			
FROM: Assistant management accountant			
Code	**Task**	**Estimated Duration**	**Required**
MH1	Visit shop and buy coffee, milk and cakes.	1 hour	Friday morning
MH2	Contact supplier and let them know that racquet Nimbus Nano is low in inventory.	15 mins	Friday morning
MH3	Assist in re-calculation value of feather shuttles now that the price of feathers has increased.	2 hours	Friday morning

JOB DESCRIPTION	
	POST DETAILS
Job Title	Management Accounts Clerk
Salary	£11,500 – £13,500
Location	Nuneaton
Reports to	Assistant Management Accountant
Date	April 20Y9

KEY RESPONSIBILITIES

- To use own initiative to deal with and react to enquiries in the absence of an Assistant Management Accountant.

- To provide administrative and clerical support to the Assistant Management Accountant, including the maintenance of the non-current asset register (fixed asset register) and calculation of depreciation.

- To undertake work as requested by the Assistant Management Accountant.

- To be aware of the importance of maintaining strict confidentiality in all aspects of work.

PERSON SPECIFICATION		
CRITERIA	**ESSENTIAL**	**DESIRABLE**
Qualifications	▪ GCSE English & Mathematics (Grade A* – C)	Undertaking AAT Level 2 qualification Willingness to undertake higher level study Level 2 Word processing Level 2 Spreadsheets
Experience	▪ Evidence of good organisational skills ▪ Basic computer skills ▪ General office procedures ▪ Competent with figures ▪ Ability to prioritise tasks	Previous accounts or clerical experience
Communication skills	▪ Evidence of successfully communicating with people at all levels ▪ Understanding of confidentiality	
Team work	▪ Knowledge and understanding of working in a team ▪ Ability to work flexibly in a team	Previous experience of working in a team
Other requirements		Current driving licence

	A	B	C
1	Employee name	Qualifying salary	NI at 12%
2	A Lot	3,600	
3	B Good	1,210	
4	C Clearly	1,550	
5	D Light	999	
6	E Bygum	2,566	
7	F Blinding	1,961	
8	G Wizz	817	

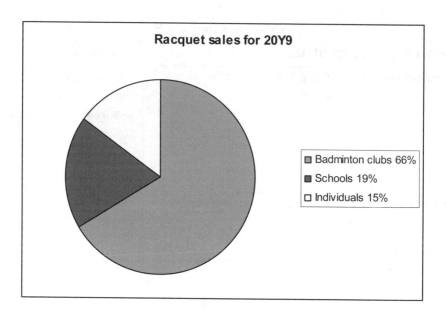

Section 1

TASK 1.1a

You have been told to have a look at the company's organisation chart but you can't find it.

    (i)   Explain what is meant by an organisation chart.

    (ii)   Identify the two reporting lines of Badders UK Ltd.

TASK 1.1b

Explain what is meant by working capital.

TASK 1.1c

Badders UK Ltd's policy on information ensures that it complies with certain legal requirements. .

    (i)   What type of legislation does it cover?

    (ii)   Explain the importance of following company policies.

TASK 1.1d

Your friend, the financial accounts clerk, usually banks the weekly cash on a Friday morning. As your friend is on holiday, the assistant financial accountant has asked you to do it. Your line manager has also asked you to do some work for Friday morning and you are not sure that you will have time to do both.

    (i)   What should you do?

    (ii)   Explain the possible consequences of not banking regularly.

TASK 1.1e

You have noticed that some of the other members of the team do not appear to get on with each other very well. You have been asked to complete a memo explaining the problems which conflict can cause to the workplace and explaining how it could be resolved.

MEMO
From:
To:　　　　Accounts department
Date:
Subject:

Task 1.2a

You have been looking at a presentation which the assistant management accountant is preparing. The pie chart looks fine but it would be helpful if there were some numbers. These appear to have been missed off. Using the percentages from the pie chart, fill in the sales figures below.

	Sales
	£
Badminton clubs	
Schools	
Individuals	
Total	5,912,000

TASK 1.2b

You meet your friend, the financial accounts clerk, for a drink after work on Monday to ask about his holiday. He tells you that the holiday was good but now he has fallen behind on his work and doesn't really know where to begin tomorrow morning. You tell him to do the important tasks first and say that you will help him with the urgent tasks. Explain to him the difference between urgent tasks and important tasks.

TASK 1.2c

Give two examples of planning aids which are used by most employees in the workplace.

SECTION 2

TASK 2.1a

Explain the benefits of employee Continuous Professional Development (CPD) to an **organisation**.

TASK 2.1b

The finance director has said that there is no budget available for Continuous Professional Development (CPD) training courses. Several people are extremely worried about this because they have to complete CPD as part of their professional accountancy qualification. Suggest three ways of obtaining CPD which will not involve expensive training courses.

TASK 2.1c

Review the job description and person specification for your job against your skills and identify two strengths and two weaknesses you possess.

STRENGTHS	WEAKNESSES
1.	1.
2.	2.

TASK 2.1d

Focusing on the weaknesses identified in Task 2.1c, the current requirements in the job description and person specification and your future career aspirations, identify at least four further development needs using the Personal Development Plan (PDP) pro forma on the following page.

PERSONAL DEVELOPMENT PLAN FOR THE FORTHCOMING YEAR

Name: _____

Date: _____

What do I want/ need to learn?	What will I do to achieve the learning need?	What resources or support will I need?	Target date for completion	With whom and when will this be reviewed?
1. AAT Level 2 Cert. in Accounting	Attend my training provider	Time to revise for my exams	May 20X1	Assistant management accountant at review
2.				
3.				
4.				
5.				
6.				
7.				

TASK 2.1e

You have recently been sitting with Fred Granger from payroll. Fred and the payroll team have made you feel very welcome. He has been showing you how the payroll system works and you have viewed confidential information about salaries and taxes. You have been checking some of the figures on a large complicated spreadsheet. Fred had to show you some new spreadsheet skills. You thoroughly enjoyed your time in the payroll department. Some people have criticised you for wasting time when payroll is not your job.

(i)   Calculate the missing figures on the spreadsheet extract (given above). Give your answers to the nearest whole pound.

(ii)   Write a report explaining the benefits to you of having spent time work-shadowing Fred. Attach your spreadsheet extract as an appendix to your report.

REPORT on _____

TO: _____

FROM: _____

DATE: _____

AAT PRACTICE ASSESSMENT – ANSWERS

TASK 1.1a

Organisation chart

An organisation chart is used to show the structure of an organisation or function. Vertical lines link different levels and show who works for who (known as the reporting lines). Your supervisor or line manager is your direct superior in the line. Horizontal lines link positions at the same level of the organisation.

Reporting lines

Management Accounts Clerk – Assistant Management Accountant – Management Accountant – Finance Director

Financial Accounts Clerk – Assistant Financial Accountant – Financial Accountant – Finance Director

TASK 1.1b

Working capital is the day-to-day finance required for operational activities. It is the finance that keeps the business running. It comprises:

Inventory (stock) + Receivables (debtors) + Cash – Payables (creditors) - Overdrafts

TASK 1.1c

Information policy

The information policy covers data protection legislation.

Importance of following company policy

It is important to follow company policies for several reasons. Firstly, to support efficient working by avoiding 'reinventing the wheel' for every task. Secondly, to support compliance with law and regulation. For example, the information policy covers the Data Protection Act. Thirdly, to support people, for example in the case of health and safety and security. Finally, policies often protect the finance, property, information and other assets of the organisation. Policies are therefore extremely important to an organisation.

TASK 1.1d

(i) If you think that you will not be able to meet a deadline then you must inform the person you report to (the assistant management accountant) as soon as possible. The assistant management accountant should take it up with the assistant financial accountant who has given you the extra work. They should decide between them how to resolve the problem.

(ii) The accounting function must closely monitor the cash balances of the business in order to ensure the solvency of the organisation. It must be able to meet its short-term and long-term debts as they fall due. Regular banking plays a vital part in ensuring that the business stays solvent.

TASK 1.1e

MEMO

From: Jo Bloggs, Management Accounts Clerk
To: Accounts department
Date: 6th April 20X1
Subject: Team work

Dear Team,

In any working relationship or team, there are bound to be conflicts occasionally. This could be due to differences in personality, differences in working styles, competition between groups, unfair treatment or even general workload stress.

Effects of unresolved conflict and dissatisfaction

If conflict and dissatisfaction are allowed to go unresolved, or to get worse, they can have a negative impact on the functioning and effectiveness of the team.

Individuals may become resentful, demotivated and uncooperative. Unresolved conflict between individuals can result in reduced communication, coordination and cooperation between them. Conflict between individuals may split the team and make rivalry and hostility even worse. It is clear that unresolved conflict can significantly interfere with team working.

Dealing with dissatisfaction and conflicts

If you have a problem working with someone you might initially attempt direct, informal discussion with the person concerned. Getting the problem out in the open may help to clear up any misunderstandings.

Problems of incompatible working styles or excessive work demands are matters which can be taken up with your line manager.

If the conflict is with someone in authority over you, you may have to discuss the matter with someone higher up in the organisation. This is probably best dealt with using more formal channels called grievance procedures (see the company policy book).

Jo Bloggs

TASK 1.2a

	Sales
	£
Badminton clubs	3,901,920
Schools	1,123,280
Individuals	886,800
Total	5,912,000

TASK 1.2b

Urgent tasks are those for which there is an imminent deadline. For example, producing a schedule of this months sales figures for the financial accountant for a meeting this afternoon.

Important tasks are tasks which have significant potential impacts on task fulfilment, other employees or the organisation. For example, the checking of purchase invoices to goods received notes and the opening of the morning post.

TASK 1.2c

'To do' list

Diary

(You may have thought of other equally valid suggestions such as email reminders, schedules etc but remember that you only need to give two examples.)

SECTION 2

TASK 2.1a

All professional bodies require their members to keep their technical knowledge up-to-date, as a condition of membership. All members of the accounts team are therefore bound to complete a certain number of hours of CPD or they will not be able to continue as members of their professional body. Completing CPD and retaining their membership has several benefits. Employees will stay up-to-date with the latest skills and knowledge required to do their job. This will mean that they will be better equipped to perform their job well. Less supervision may be required, productivity may increase, risks of errors may be reduced and compliance with laws and regulations will be more likely. It can also act as a motivational tool as employees see that the employer values their qualification. Additionally, providing CPD may enhance the ability of the organisation to recruit and retain professionally qualified staff.

TASK 2.1b

1 The internet

2 Books
3 Colleagues

(You may have thought of other equally valid suggestions but remember that you only need to list three.)

TASK 2.1c

You should assess your own real-life skills against those identified in the person specification and also the requirements of the job description.

TASK 2.1d

You are required to make sensible suggestions related to the current role as Management Accounts Clerk as described and also your own (real life) career aspirations. Timescales should also be considered.

TASK 2.1e

	A	B	C
1	Employee name	Qualifying salary	NI at 12%
2	A Lot	3,600	432
3	B Good	1,210	145
4	C Clearly	1,550	186
5	D Light	999	120
6	E Bygum	2,566	308
7	F Blinding	1,961	235
8	G Wizz	817	98

REPORT on the benefits of shadow-working with payroll

TO: Assistant management accountant

FROM: Jo Bloggs

DATE: 2nd July 20X0

I   Introduction

I have recently spent some time working with Fred Granger in the payroll department. Although payroll is not part of my day-to-day job, the experience has been extremely valuable. The purpose of this report is to explain the benefits I have received.

2   Covering holiday and sick leave

When I joined Badders UK Ltd, the management accountant explained that I would have to help out with other areas of the business to cover absences. Up until now I had had no experience in the payroll department and so was not able to provide this cover. Now that Fred has shown me what to do I will be happy and confident to provide cover when necessary.

3   Spreadsheet skills

The spreadsheet that Fred showed me was far more complicated than anything that I had dealt with before. Working on it has improved my spreadsheet skills greatly and I may be able to incorporate these skills into my every day work. I should also be to count this as CPD.

4   Teamwork and communication

Spending time in the payroll department has helped me to get to know the payroll staff. This can only help to improve communication between the payroll team and the accounts team in the future. I also feel extremely motivated after the warm welcome that I received from the payroll department.

5   Conclusion

The experience has been invaluable. I feel able to perform my job to the best of my abilities and I feel extremely motivated.

Appendices:

Appendix 1: Spreadsheet extract (attached)

INDEX

Accounting function, 8
Accounting information, 12
Accuracy, 47, 58
Action plan, 103
Addition, 52
Appendix, 68
Assertive communication, 122
Assistance, 121
Authorisations, 36
Authority, 24
Averages, 56

Bar charts, 72
Budgets, 13

Career goals, 141
Cash flow, 13
Chain of command, 24
Changes in priority, 97
Clear desk policy, 33
Codes of Practice, 18
Collaboration, 118
Commitments, 118
Communication, 24, 44, 106, 118
Communication policies, 65
Compliance, 14, 16
Confidentiality, 33, 107
Conflict, 123, 126
Conflict of priorities, 99
Continuing professional development, 134
Co-ordination, 116, 118
Corporate governance, 17
Corporate identity, 51
Corporate image, 51
Cross-functional teams, 24

Data protection, 17
Data security, 33, 34
Document retention, 35
Deadlines, 35, 118, 120
Debts, 14
Departmental deadlines, 35, 120

Departments, 24
Designated signatories, 37
Development, 134
Diagrams, 50, 71
Diary, 100
Dissatisfactions, 123, 125
Division, 53

Efficiency, 13
Email, 64, 82
Equal opportunity, 17, 125
Escalation, 127
Experiential learning, 144

Feedback, 45, 118, 141
Financial accounting, 9
Financial functions, 11
Financial statements, 9, 35
Formality, 52
Fractions, 53

Gantt chart, 100
Grievance, 128
Grievance procedure, 128

Health and safety, 17, 30
HM Revenue and Customs, 10, 35
House style, 65, 78

Important tasks, 94
Informal report, 64, 67
Information, 11
Information flows, 10
Intellectual property, 17
Internet, 144

Jargon, 47
Job description, 90, 136

KISS, 50

Learning needs, 136
Legal and regulatory requirements, 14
Letter, 64, 75
Letterheads, 75
Line functions, 8
Line graphs, 73
Line manager, 24, 27, 147

Management accounting, 9
Means of communication, 45
Memo, 64, 80
Methods of communication, 64
Monitoring, 104, 145
Motivation, 116
Multiplication, 53

Negotiation, 126
Numeracy skills, 52

Objectives, 118, 142
Organisation charts, 24
Organisation structure, 24

PASS, 48
Payroll function, 10
Percentages, 54
Performance appraisal, 146
Person specification, 136
Personal Development Journal, 140
Personal Development Plan, 146
Personal effects, 33
Phishing, 69
Pie charts, 72
Planning aids, 99
Policies, 29
Presentation, 50
Prioritising, 95
Procedures, 29, 106
Professional bodies, 18, 134
Professionalism, 50
Project manager, 27
Publications, 144

Recording CPD activity, 148
Regulatory bodies, 18
Reporting lines, 27
Review, 145
Rounding, 55

Routine tasks, 92
Rules, 30

Salutations, 78
Scenario, 2
Schedules, 100
Scheduling, 98
Security, 31
Seeking assistance, 105
Set priorities, 92
SMART, 142
Solvency, 14
Sources of CPD, 143
Staff functions, 8
Storage of data, 34
Strengths and weaknesses, 139
Styles of communication, 51
Subject line, 83
Subtraction, 52
Support, 121

Tables, 71
Tasks, 2
Team, 116
Team roles, 117
Team working, 117
Technical briefings, 143
Time management, 92
Timetable, 100
To Do List, 99
Training, 134
Training courses, 143

Unexpected tasks, 94
Urgency, 92
Urgent tasks, 94

Win win model, 126
Work area, 107
Work area, 32
Working capital, 13
Working hours, 32
Working practice, 106

REVIEW FORM

How have you used this Workbook?
(Tick one box only)

☐ Home study

☐ On a course_____

☐ Other _____

Why did you decide to purchase this Workbook?
(Tick one box only)

☐ Have used BPP Texts in the past

☐ Recommendation by friend/colleague

☐ Recommendation by a college lecturer

☐ Saw advertising

☐ Other _____

During the past six months do you recall seeing/receiving either of the following?
(Tick as many boxes as are relevant)

☐ Our advertisement in Accounting Technician

☐ Our Publishing Catalogue

Which (if any) aspects of our advertising do you think are useful?
(Tick as many boxes as are relevant)

☐ Prices and publication dates of new editions

☐ Information on Text content

☐ Details of our free online offering

☐ None of the above

Your ratings, comments and suggestions would be appreciated on the following areas of this Workbook.

	Very useful	Useful	Not useful
Introductory section	☐	☐	☐
Quality of explanations	☐	☐	☐
How it works	☐	☐	☐
Chapter tasks	☐	☐	☐
Chapter Overviews	☐	☐	☐
Test your learning	☐	☐	☐
Index	☐	☐	☐

	Excellent	Good	Adequate	Poor
Overall opinion of this Workbook	☐	☐	☐	☐

Do you intend to continue using BPP Products?   ☐ Yes   ☐ No

Please note any further comments and suggestions/errors on the reverse of this page. The author of this edition can be e-mailed at: suedexter@bpp.com

Please return to: Sue Dexter, Publishing Director, BPP Learning Media Ltd, FREEPOST, London, W12 8BR.

REVIEW FORM (continued)

TELL US WHAT YOU THINK

Please note any further comments and suggestions/errors below.